# PRODUCTS LIABILITY

## IN A NUTSHELL

Fourth Edition

By

### JERRY J. PHILLIPS
W. P. Toms Professor of Law,
University of Tennessee

ST. PAUL, MINN.
WEST PUBLISHING CO.
1993

COPYRIGHT © 1974, 1981, 1988 WEST PUBLISHING CO.
COPYRIGHT © 1993 By WEST PUBLISHING CO.
610 Opperman Drive
P.O. Box 64526
St. Paul, MN 55164–0526
1–800–328–9352

**Library of Congress Cataloging-in-Publication Data**
Phillips, Jerry J., 1935-
    Products liability in a nutshell / by Jerry J. Phillips. — 4th
ed.
        p.     cm. — (Nutshell series)
    Includes index.
    ISBN 0–314–02252–X
    1. Products liability—United States.   I. Title.   II. Series.
KF1296.Z9P48   1993
346.7303'8—dc20
[347.30638]                                          93–1654
                                                       CIP

**ISBN** 0–314–02252–X

 *TEXT IS PRINTED ON 10% POST CONSUMER RECYCLED PAPER*

Phillips, Prod.Liab. 4th Ed. NS
1st Reprint—1995

To
Anne, Sherman
and Dorothy

*

# PREFACE

Products liability has become a bellwether for tort law. It carries forward the development of strict liability from its origins in res ipsa loquitur, vicarious liability, warranty, and abnormally dangerous activities. It leads in exploring the problems of multiple causation and epidemiological cause. It poses the major issues concerning mass tort litigation, and the methods for handling such widespread related claims.

There have been a number of proposals and extensive discussion regarding the possibility of devising alternative dispute-resolution methods for tort law, including products liability. Many such mechanisms are already in place, in the form of workers' compensation, no-fault auto insurance, medicare and medicaid, and private health insurance plans. Such alternative compensation devices may never provide a complete or satisfactory substitute for the tort law remedy, however, which may remain necessary to provide a sense of vindication and fairness that are unlikely to be found in administrative and other non-adversarial forms of compensation.

During the mid-1970s and mid-1980s a number of states enacted products liability statutes generally retrenching on consumers' interests in this area. These statutes affect such matters as damages, statutes of repose, state of the art, joint liability, statutory compliance, and the like. They were enacted in response to a perceived liability and insurance-availability crisis. Time will tell whether they will withstand scrutiny. Repeated efforts have been unsuccessful in obtaining passage of a federal products liability statute. Whenever consulting the law of a particular state, the lawyer and law student should of course determine whether that state has adopted any special products liability statutory enactments.

In this Nutshell I attempt not only to state the established rules of products liability law, but also to explain the interrelation of those rules and other problems that often arise in their application. I believe that this kind of approach to the law will benefit the student and practitioner more than just a black-letter statement. Neither the student nor the lawyer is very often asked only to state a rule of law. The person asking also wants to know how the rule is applied, what are the reasons for the rule, and how the rule should be distinguished from other apparently closely related rules. That person usually asks about questions of procedure and strategy, about common sense issues of what is practical and workable, and about broad questions of fairness. If the lawyer and law student are not prepared to address these questions, they are not prepared to practice law. I have tried to address these kinds of questions in this book.

It will be readily apparent to anyone who reads this book that there is a large amount of overlapping of issues. Overlap — a characteristic of many areas of the law — is particularly evident in products liability owing to the numerous related ideological bases of the subject matter, as well as to the constantly developing law in this area. While the problem of overlap works against clarity, it provides a richness of warp and woof that keeps the subject alive and vital.

An issue related to overlapping is that of ambiguity. It is not uncommon to have two or more positions on most propositions of law, and products law certainly shares that condition in abundance. In addition, many of the areas of products law remain shadowy and uncertain. This uncertainty is attributable to the vibrant, developing nature of the subject. At first blush this characteristic may be cold comfort to many students, but I hope they will come to appreciate it as an element that sustains freedom and independence of thought.

No one would have predicted the course of development that the law of products liability would take when *Greenman v. Yuba Power Products* was decided in 1963. In much the same way, no one can predict with confidence what products law will look like in the first half of the twenty-first century — whose beginning is upon us. Judging from past experience, however, one thing seems sure. The law will continue to develop, in a genuine effort to meet the demands for quality and safety that are a hallmark of our consumer-oriented society.

JERRY J. PHILLIPS

Knoxville, Tennessee
January 1993

*

# OUTLINE

# TABLE OF CASES

**References are to Pages**

---

## A

XV

# B

XVIII

# C

# D

# E

# G

# H

# I

# J

# K

# L

# N

# O

# P

*TABLE OF CASES*

# R

# S

# T

# W

# Y

# Z

# PRODUCTS LIABILITY

## IN A NUTSHELL

Fourth Edition

*

# CHAPTER I

# DEFINITION AND SCOPE
## A. WHAT IS A PRODUCT?

A product is usually thought of as tangible personal property—as a good, or chattel. The term is more or less synonymous with "goods" as used in the UCC § 2–105(1). Indeed, the law of products liability has its origins in the sales article of the Uniform Sales Act, now the Uniform Commercial Code, as well as in the common law of torts.

Products liability has extended beyond tangible goods, however, to include intangibles such as electricity after it has been delivered to the consumer. Houston Lighting & Power Co. v. Reynolds (1988). In Bradley v. American Smelting and Refining Co. (1985), where the court found trespass and nuisance resulting from the invasion of microscopic particles from defendant's copper smelting plant onto plaintiff's land, the court said, "the now famous equation of $E = MC^2$ has taught us that mass and energy are equivalents." Products law has been applied to natural products, such as a pet skunk, Sease v. Taylor's Pets (1985) (pet shop strictly liable for injuries resulting from the sale of a rabid skunk). It has been applied to writings such as a mass-produced aircraft navigational

1

chart, Saloomey v. Jeppesen & Co. (1983), and to real estate fixtures such as a house, Blagg v. Fred Hunt Co., Inc. (1981).

In the case of writings, there may be constitutional limitations on the imposition of liability. For example, in Alm v. Van Nostrand Reinhold Co., Inc. (1985) the court refused to impose liability for injuries resulting from negligent misrepresentation against the publisher of a "how-to" toolmaking book, because the burden of liability would be too great even if it were constitutionally permissible under the first amendment of the U.S. Constitution. See also Birmingham v. Fodor's Travel Publications, Inc. (1992) (no negligence or strict liability of a book publisher). In the case of real estate construction, there may be concern about extending the products doctrine of strict liability to real estate and to service transactions. Milam v. Midland Corp. (1984) (residential developer not strictly liable for building dangerous street—not a product); Thibos v. Pacific Gas & Elec. Co. (1986) (street lighting furnished by defendant utility was a "service" rather than a "product"). The court in Snyder v. ISC Alloys, Inc. (1991) held that the supplier of plans for the design of a zinc dust plant could not be found strictly liable since the plans were not a product, but could be liable in negligence for foreseeable risks associated with the design. With regard to animals, there may be a reluctance to impose liability because of the difficulties of proving causation. Latham v. Wal–Mart

Stores, Inc. (1991) (psittacosis from diseased parrot).

In deciding whether the law of products liability should apply, the issue should not be restricted to the inquiry of whether a product is involved. Rather, the inquiry should also be directed to whether or not the defendant is in the best position to spread the loss and prevent injuries, and to other policy concerns such as freedom of speech and the difficulties of proof.

## B.  WHAT IS A DEFECT?
### 1.  IN GENERAL

It is generally said that the reason for imposing liability against a product supplier for injuries resulting from a product is because the product is supplied in a defective condition.  This statement may be too broad, since there are situations in which there is nothing wrong with the product and yet the law of products liability applies.  Thus a supplier may be liable for the negligent entrustment of a sound product, Moning v. Alfono (1977) (negligent supply of slingshot to minor), for misstatements regarding a product's capabilities, Baxter v. Ford Motor Co. (1934) (windshield alleged to be shatterproof), or for the supply of a product that constitutes an abnormally dangerous activity, Siegler v. Kuhlman (1972) (tank truck transport of gasoline).  For the most part, however, proof that the product was defective when it left the defendant's hands is a sine qua non to recovery. See Gann v. International Harvester Co. (1991) ("Absent showing a defective, unreasonably dangerous product, the plaintiff could not establish a case of negligence in any event.") it may be that the exceptions (negligent entrustment, misrepresentation, abnormally dangerous activities) will someday swallow the rule that requires proof of defect, and in that event the focus of liability will shift either to proof of fault or proof of causation. Alternatively, it may be argued (as noted below with regard to misrepresentation) that a product that is harmful—because of defendant's negligence, misrepresentation, or abnormally dangerous conduct—is a defective product in the context of its use.

Determining defectiveness is one of the more difficult problems in products liability, particularly in design litigation. The issue implicates questions of the proper scope of the strict liability doctrine, and the overlapping definitions of physical and conceptual views of defectiveness.

### 2.   TYPES OF DEFECT AND THEIR INTERRELATION

It is often said that there are three types of product defects: 1) manufacturing or production flaws, 2) design defects, and 3) defective warnings or instructions. To these three some commentators add a fourth category, 4) misrepresentation. Others say that misrepresentation is not a defect, since there is nothing wrong with the product itself. This is debatable, since there may likewise be nothing physically wrong with a product lacking adequate warnings. A mislabeled (i.e., misrepresented) product may be just as dangerous as one containing an inadequate warning.

Some writers treat warning defects as a type of design defect. The rationale for doing this is at least twofold. One is that a warning inadequacy, like a design inadequacy, is usually characteristic of a whole line of products, while a production or manufacturing flaw is usually random and atypical of the product. Another is that many—perhaps a majority—of the courts say that strict liability is no different from (or is the same as) negligence in the case of both design and warning defects, while fault is generally irrelevant in determining production flaws. Moreover, there are instances in which design and warning flaws meld, as for example in Pike v. Frank G. Hough Co. (1970), where a paydozer was alleged to be defective because of the lack of rear view mirrors and backup warning signals. Such mirrors and signals are warnings that would require physical redesign of the product, and not just the attachment of written warning labels on the product.

The distinction between production and design defects is likewise not clear on close scrutiny. It cannot be based on intention (intentional design, versus inadvertent production defect), because many design deficiencies are unintentional while many production and testing standards that result in occasional errors are consciously selected to keep down costs. While production flaws tend to be random, and design characteristics generic, this distinction also does not consistently hold true. Different types of use will cause the same kinds of metal not to withstand stresses, resulting in random failures. Also, raw pork for example occasionally contains trichinae, but this is because of a design decision not to precook or freeze the meat or to test for trichinae.

The real question is why is it important to distinguish between production and design defects in the first place? If it is because strict liability is only imposed for production defects, as opposed to design defects, there still remains the question of why this should be so? It may be because production defects so clearly fall below ordinary consumer expectations that fault is assumed; we all know that a properly prepared bottle of coke should not contain a mouse. But it does not follow that the presence of the mouse is necessarily the result of fault. Thus, baby chicks may be randomly infected with avian leukosis, as in Vlases v. Montgomery Ward & Co. (1967), making them as unacceptable as a coke containing a mouse, although it was undisputed that avian leukosis is undetectable and untreatable in newborn chicks; yet the supplier in *Vlases* was held strictly liable for the damages resulting from the disease.

Moreover, as will be discussed later, the doctrine of unavoidably unsafe products—which apparently applies to production flaws as well as design defects, so as to prohibit the imposition of strict liability—throws the whole distinction between production and design flaws into disarray insofar as that distinction turns on the applicability of strict liability. These problems suggest that future cases will not draw a bright line between production and design flaws, but they do not indicate whether the movement in both areas will be toward strict liability or a fault-based standard of liability.

A case illustrating the overlap of design and production defects is Faucett v. Ingersoll–Rand Mining & Machinery Co. (1992). The plaintiff there was injured when he slipped on hydraulic fuel that had leaked into the operator's department of a roof-bolter machine manufactured by the defendant. Plaintiff's expert testified that such leaks were "virtually inevitable at some point in time," but that the risk could be eliminated at slight cost by installing a floor grating or by putting the hydraulic valve outside the operator department. The expert also testified that "the fittings on the hosing" of the hydraulic system "were improper for mining conditions." The court held the plaintiff was entitled to have a jury determine whether the product was unreasonably dangerous and defective. One would likely assume that such oil leakage would be a random occurrence, or a production flaw, but its "virtual inevitability" suggests that the product had a design flaw that was typical of the whole product line. Whether the problem is viewed as one of production or design, however, the same method would be used here to determine the product's defectiveness.  See also Bryan v. John Bean Div. of FMC Corp. (1978), given in Chapter VII, Sec. B.

Finally, a misrepresentation is not clearly distinguishable from other types of product defects, for a number of reasons.  First, the product itself may carry express representations.  In Hochberg v. O'Donnell's Restaurant (1971), the court held that the plaintiff could recover for a broken tooth when he bit down on an unpitted olive in a martini, thinking it was pitted because he saw a "hole in one end of an olive and therefore assumed it had been pitted."  Plaintiff conceded that "if he had not seen the hole in one end of the olive his case would be 'extremely tenuous' ", apparently because there was no custom of serving martinis only with pitted olives.  We may assume that the defect here was one of production, since the olive should have been pitted (owing to the hole) but was not.  The case also fits neatly into the category of misrepresentation.  The plaintiff must have thought he could not recover for injury resulting from a manufacturing or production flaw, because there was no ordinary consumer expectation that the olive would be pitted.  Had there been such an expectation, then he could have recovered for a production defect as well as for misrepresentation.

Second, the product itself, just from its general appearance, may imply safety.  Justice Traynor, speaking for the majority in Greenman v. Yuba Power Products, Inc. (1963), said that a combination power tool with inadequate set screws could be found defective because "[i]mplicit in the machine's presence on the market ... was a representation that it would safely do the jobs for which it was built." The defect here, presumably one of design, was also viewed by the court as one of implied misrepresentation because of the product's appearance.

Third, the defects of inadequate warning and of misrepresentation are often intimately intertwined because of countervailing statements that accompany a warning. Thus, a "caution" against inhaling the fumes of carbon tetrachloride, and a cautionary direction to "use only in well ventilated places", were counteracted in Maize v. Atlantic Ref. Co. (1945) by the prominently displayed representation "Safety–Kleen" on the label of the product, excluding from the user's mind "that 'provident fear' which has been characterized as 'the mother of safety'."

Almost all courts hold that a products liability action for misrepresentation can be tried in strict liability—although an action for negligent or fraudulent misrepresentation can of course also be brought if the facts warrant such claims. Insofar, therefore, as innocent misrepresentation overlaps with design and warning defects, and production defects involving unavoidably unsafe products, a count of misrepresentation may convert the action from one of fault to strict liability. Owing to the pervasiveness of advertisements that accompany the sale of most modern products, a misrepresentation claim based on advertising may be available in many products liability suits.

## 3.   CONCEPTUAL STANDARDS FOR DETERMINING DEFECTIVENESS

### a.   In General

There are several definitions that may be used to describe each of the types of defects (design, warning and production flaws) discussed in the previous section. Misrepresentations often stand on a different footing, owing to the presence of reliance on express statements. The failure of the courts to settle on a single definition of defect for design, warning and production flaws indicates the fluidity of the law in this area, as well as the uncertainty regarding the proper scope of the law of products liability.

It should be noted that the term "defect" is used herein to describe generically the kinds and definitions of things that courts find to be actionably wrong with products when they leave the seller's hands. In the decisions, however, the courts sometimes distinguish between defectiveness and unreasonable danger. Moreover, they distinguish between dangerously defective products and unmerchantable products, particularly where only economic loss is involved. These distinctions will be discussed in detail hereafter.

## b. Consumer Expectations

A common and perhaps the prevailing definition of product unsatisfactoriness is that of "unreasonable danger", given in comment *i* of the Rest. 2d Torts § 402A: "The article sold must be dangerous to an extent beyond that which would be contemplated by the ordinary consumer who purchases it, with the ordinary knowledge common to the community as to its characteristics." This standard of implied ordinary consumer expectations is similar to that of merchantability, as defined in the sales article of the UCC, with the difference that the Code does not require the goods to be "dangerous" as a condition to unmerchantability. The central provision of the implied warranty of merchantability is the statement that goods, to be merchantable, must be at least such as "are fit for the ordinary purposes for which such goods are used." UCC § 2–314(2)(c).

The standard of implied ordinary consumer expectations is unnecessary in the case of misrepresentation. The representation itself establishes the consumer's expectations—which may be ordinary or special, depending on the content of the representation.

The standard of ordinary consumer expectations works well for many production defects, since the random departure can often be measured against the norm as representative of ordinary expectations. The average consumer can easily determine, for example, that ground glass in food does not meet ordinary expectations. The ordinary consumer test may also work well for many warning situations, since the consumer—just as the medical patient in the context of informed consent—often knows what he would like to be warned about.

Not all warning- and production-defect cases fall within the realm of ordinary expectations, however. Thus in the case of warnings to doctors, expert testimony may be required where matters are involved "with respect to which a layman can have no knowledge at all." Hill v. Squibb & Sons, E.R. (1979). The same can be true of production defects. Expert evidence may be required to establish how much impact the metal of a truck wheel can withstand, as in Heaton v. Ford Motor Co. (1967), regardless of whether the alleged defect is one of production or design. In design cases generally, it is usual for expert evidence to be required to establish defectiveness.

Some have criticized the ordinary consumer expectations test as not being useful when the danger is obvious, since in that situation the consumer cannot expect the product to be safe. So in Higgs v. General Motors Corp. (1985) the court held the plaintiffs did not state a cause of action against the defendant car manufacturer for failure to equip its cars with air bags, since "the plaintiffs as 'ordinary consumers' did not expect air bags to pop out of the dash." This result is questionable, in view of the modern trend to treat obviousness of danger as only one factor to be considered by the fact finder in determining whether a product is defective. Moreover, a consumer can certainly expect that a product should be safe even though it evidently is not.

Another criticism sometimes leveled against the consumer expectation test is that it is unhelpful in the case of a complicated product, since the consumer lacks any basis for determining how safe the product should be. The basis of expectation here is however typically furnished by expert testimony, whether the suit is brought in strict liability or in negligence. Thus in Karns v. Emerson Elec. Co. (1987) an expert was permitted to testify that defendant's product was "unreasonably dangerous beyond the expectation of the average user." Ordinary consumer expectations, as well as the standard of care of a reasonable person, can be informed by expert witness evidence, but that evidence does not make the expectations of either the ordinary consumer or the reasonable person any less relevant or outcome-determinative.

### c. Presumed Seller Knowledge

Another test of defectiveness sometimes used is that of presumed seller knowledge: would the seller be negligent in placing a product on the market *if he had knowledge of its harmful or dangerous condition?* As can be seen, this definition contains a standard of strict liability, as well as one of defectiveness, since it assumes the seller's knowledge of a product's condition even though there may be no such knowledge or reason to know.

The court in Phillips v. Kimwood Machine Co. (1974) found no necessary inconsistency between the consumer-expectation and the seller-assumed-knowledge tests, since "each turns on foreseeable risks. They are two sides of the same standard. A product is defective and unreasonably dangerous when a reasonable seller would not sell the product if he knew of the risks involved or if the risks are greater than a reasonable buyer would expect.... [A] seller acting reasonably would be selling the same product which a reasonable consumer believes he is purchasing." This similarity does not exist, however, where the seller-oriented test turns on seller assumed knowledge but the consumer-oriented test turns on the consumer's actual knowledge or reason to know.

The seller-oriented test is apparently one of imputed general knowledge, rather than specific knowledge about each particular product. If it were specific knowledge, the seller could never reasonably market a product with a latent manufacturing flaw. For example, a blood bank could never reasonably market a pint of blood knowing that it contained the hepatitis virus. It would reasonably market units of blood, however, with the generalized knowledge that some unknown random few of those units contain the virus, since the benefits would outweigh the risk.

This risk-benefit approach to production-defect cases brings these cases closely in line conceptually with the standard for judging cases of design and warning defects. This is because usually something like a risk-benefit approach is used in these latter cases.

Strict liability cases based on innocent (as opposed to negligent or reckless) misrepresentation do not involve a risk-benefit analysis. It is enough here that a material statement about the product is made, and that it proves false with resulting proximate harm to the plaintiff.

Whether there may be first amendment constitutional limitations on liability for misrepresentation raises the same questions indicated in the first section of this chapter dealing with the liability of book publishers. The defamation case of Dun & Bradstreet, Inc. v. Greenmoss Builders, Inc. (1985) indicates that there may be no free speech limitations on purely commercial speech concerning private parties and matters of private concern, but it is unclear how this decision would apply to products litigation.

## d.   Risk–Benefit Balancing

A number of courts, perhaps a majority, use a risk-benefit analysis to determine defectiveness, particularly in design cases. A straightforward negligence analysis is more common in warning cases. A test based on consumer expectations is often used in production-defect cases, as in Rix v. General Motors Corp. (1986)—except with regard to unavoidably unsafe products. Defectiveness for purposes of misrepresentation in strict liability, as already noted, usually requires only a showing of a product representation that proves false and causes expectable injury to the plaintiff.

Risk-benefit can be understood as essentially the same thing as risk-utility. The issue is phrased in terms of whether the cost of making a safer product is greater or less than the risk or danger from the product in its present condition. If the cost of making the change is greater than the risk created by not making the change, then the benefit or utility of keeping the product as is outweighs the risk and the product is not defective. If on the other hand the cost is less than the risk, then the benefit or utility of not making the change is outweighed by the risk and the product in its unchanged condition is defective.

Another way of phrasing the test is in terms of risk vs. cost or burden. Is the risk of danger greater than the cost or burden of eliminating that danger? If it is, the product is defective. If on the other hand the burden of eliminating the danger is greater than the risk of the danger, then the product's benefit or utility outweighs its danger and therefore the product is not defective.

This abstract formulation can better be understood by examples. Aboveground utility poles along the roadside will result in a statistically predictable number of accidents, but a municipality might determine that the cost of placing electrical lines underground (or the utility of leaving them above ground) is greater than the accident risk. Walking to work may be less dangerous than riding, but the benefit or utility of riding (or the burden of walking) may outweigh the risk. If the walk is short, on the other hand, the burden of walking might be less or the utility greater than the risk of riding.

Burden and utility may be opposite sides of the same coin, where the burden of correcting a product condition reduces its utility. In the more desirable outcome, the burden of correction will both increase the product's utility and reduce its risk.

When assessing the cost or difficulty of making a change, the courts are not in agreement in defining how cost is to be measured. Some, as in Prentis v. Yale Mfg. Co. (1984), say that the standard for determining defective design is simply one of negligence. Should the defendant reasonably have known of the product's danger and of a reasonable way to eliminate that danger? Other courts, as in Dart v. Wiebe Mfg., Inc. (1985), say that risk-benefit is not the same as negligence because, for the former, knowledge or know-how that is available at the time of trial is relevant even if it were not available when the product was manufactured.

Normally, in order to establish strict liability for an unreasonably dangerous design, said the court in Kallio v. Ford Motor Co. (1986), the plaintiff must present evidence of a feasible, alternative safer design. This requires more than a showing of the "technical possibility" of a safer design. In Owens v. Allis–Chalmers Corp. (1982), the court said that in making out a prima facie case of design defect the plaintiff must show the gravity of harm, the utility of a modified (i.e. redesigned) product, any other dangers associated with the modification, and the cost of making the modification.

A common standard used for determining risk-benefit is the seven factors proposed by Dean John Wade, as set forth in Roach v. Kononen (1974). These are: 1) the usefulness and desirability of the product; 2) the likelihood and probable seriousness of injury from the product; 3) the availability of a substitute product that would meet the same need and not be as unsafe; 4) the manufacturer's ability to eliminate the danger without impairing usefulness or making the product too expensive; 5) the user's ability to avoid the danger; 6) the user's anticipated awareness of the danger; and 7) the feasibility on the part of the manufacturer of spreading the risk of loss by pricing or insurance.

Not all courts follow the risk-utility approach in products litigation. The court in Lester v. Magic Chef, Inc. (1982) chose the consumer-expectation test over that of risk-utility. In Knitz v. Minster

Machine Co. (1982), the court held that the plaintiff could rely on consumer expectations in a design case, and if there were none, *then* on a risk-benefit analysis. California, in Barker v. Lull Engineering Co., Inc. (1978), held that the plaintiff has the option of relying on either the ordinary-consumer test or the risk-benefit test. If plaintiff chooses the latter test, she need only show that the design proximately caused her injury and then the burden shifts to the defendant to show that, "on balance, the benefits of the challenged design outweigh the risk of danger inherent in such design."

A number of cases indicate that a product may be judged unreasonably dangerous because the risk outweighs the utility even where no safer design of the product is practical or feasible. In this situation, the fact finder is in effect asked to determine whether the product should ever have been marketed. See Airco, Inc. v. Simmons First Nat. Bank, Guardian (1982) (respirator with knobs dangerously positioned). See also O'Brien v. Muskin Corp. (1983) (4–foot–deep vinyl swimming pool). This seems to have been the holding in Kelley v. R. G. Industries, Inc. (1985) ("Saturday–Night Special"), repealed by Md. Code Art. 27, § 361(h)(1) (1987). In Burks v. Firestone Tire & Rubber Co. (1981), a tire rim explosion case, the court held that a stipulation of the feasibility of a safer design did not eliminate the necessity of applying a test that balanced utility against risk of harm. In Halphen v. Johns–Manville Sales Corp. (1986), the court held that under Louisiana law asbestos may be found unreasonably dangerous per se, so that the defendant's ability to know of (and therefore remedy) the product's danger was irrelevant. A product is unreasonably dangerous per se "if a reasonable person would conclude that the danger-in-fact of the product, whether foreseeable or not, outweighs the utility of the product." The decision in *Halphen* was repealed by La. Prod. Liab. Act § 2800.56 (1988).

In Cipollone v. Liggett Group, Inc. (1986), the court held that the plaintiff could try a design defect case against a cigarette manufacturer with a risk/utility test based on "a comparison of the utility of the product with the risk of injury that it poses to the public." In making this comparison the manufacturer would not be permitted to introduce evidence of the product's profitability and the fact that "such profitability will be endangered if legal liability is found," since such evidence would "undermine the goals of greater overall economic efficiency and product safety." This decision may be overruled by a 1987 New Jersey statute providing that a product is not defectively designed if at the time of manufacture "there was not a practical and technically feasible alternative design" that would have prevented the harm without substantially impairing the product's function, unless the product is "egregiously unsafe", its danger is not known to the ordinary consumer, and the product has "little or no usefulness." N.J. Laws 1987, c. 197.

### e.  State of the Art

Risk-benefit or risk-burden balancing involves questions concerning state of the art, since the burden of eliminating a danger may be greater than the risk of that danger if the danger cannot be eliminated.  State of the art is similar to the unavoidably unsafe defense, considered in the next section, where absence of the knowledge or ability to eliminate a danger is assumed for purposes of determining if a product is unavoidably unsafe.  If, on the other hand, the jury determines as of the date of trial that a product should never have been marketed at all, neither evidence of state of the art nor of unavoidable unsafeness at the date of manufacture would be a defense.  State of the art is dealt with further in Chapter 7.E.4.

Tenn. Code Ann. § 29–28–105(b) defines state of the art as "the state of scientific and technological knowledge available to the manufacturer at the time the product was placed on the market."  In Owens–Illinois, Inc. v. Zenobia (1992) the court said that state of the art "includes all of the available knowledge on the subject at a given time, and this includes scientific, medical, engineering, and any other knowledge that may be available."  If the "given time" were the date of trial, then state of the art would be less of a defense than if the date of manufacture were used.  Many courts, however, hold that state of the art refers to the date of manufacture.  But admissibility of evidence of subsequent remedial measures, discussed in Chapter

7.D., indicates that the date of trial is the relevant time for this purpose.

In Anderson v. Owens–Corning Fiberglas Corp. (1991) the California Supreme Court held that evidence of state of the art (knowability) of the danger as of the date of manufacture was admissible in all failure to warn cases. This case essentially equates failure to warn with negligence liability. Even so, as discussed in Chapter 6.A.5., there may be a post-manufacture duty to warn or repair if the manufacturer discovers or should have discovered the product's unreasonable danger after it was marketed.

Moreover, the admissibility of date-of-manufacture knowledge or ability to make a safer product does not mean that evidence of post-manufacture knowledge of danger, or of ability to eliminate that danger, should be inadmissible in a strict liability case. Evidence of both date-of-manufacture and date-of-trial knowledge and ability could be admitted to determine defectiveness in a strict liability case.

The court in Lewis v. Coffing Hoist Div., Duff–Norton Co., Inc. (1987) said that industry custom is irrelevant for purposes of determining state of the art in a strict liability case. Other courts have held that evidence of custom is relevant to determine state of the art in a strict liability case, Chown v. USM Corp. (1980), and to show the practicality of making a safer product in such a case, McLaughlin v. Sikorsky Aircraft (1983). The

*Chown* and *McLaughlin* holdings seem reasonable, since what an industry is doing at a given time is some evidence of what that industry is capable of doing. On the other hand, if evidence of custom is admissible in a strict liability case to show state of the art at the time of manufacture, the distinction between strict liability and negligence is blurred.

### f. Unavoidably Unsafe Products

Comment *k* to the Second Restatement of Torts § 402A states:

There are some products which, in the present state of human knowledge, are quite incapable of being made safe for their intended and ordinary use. These are especially common in the field of drugs. An outstanding example is the vaccine for the Pasteur treatment of rabies, which not uncommonly leads to very serious and damaging consequences when it is injected. Since the disease itself invariably leads to a dreadful death, both the marketing and the use of the vaccine are fully justified, notwithstanding the unavoidable high degree of risk which they involve. Such a product, properly prepared, and accompanied by proper directions and warning, is not defective, nor is it *unreasonably* dangerous. The same is true of many other drugs, vaccines, and the like, many of which for this very reason cannot legally be sold except to physicians, or under the prescription of a physician. It is also true in particular of many new or experimental drugs as to which, because of the lack of time and opportunity for sufficient medical experience, there can be no assurance of safety, or perhaps even of purity of ingredients, but such experience as there is justifies the marketing and use of the drug notwithstanding a medically recognizable risk. The seller of such products, again with the qualification that they are properly prepared and marketed, and proper warning is given, where the situation calls for it, is not to be held to strict liability for unfortunate consequences attending their use, merely because he has undertaken to supply the public with an apparently useful and desirable product, attended with a known but apparently reasonable risk.

There is disagreement regarding the intended scope of this comment. Does it apply only to design defects, or does it apply to production (random) defects as well? Toner v. Lederle Labs. (1987) states that courts and commentators "universally agree" that the comment is intended to apply only to design defects. But the court in McMichael v. American Red Cross (1975) held that the comment applied to the hepatitis virus in blood, which is a random defect, and Hollinger v. Shoppers Paradise of New Jersey, Inc. (1975) indicated that it applied to the occasional trichinous pork as well.

Another issue is whether the comment applies to unknowable dangers, or only to known but unpreventable dangers. If only to the latter, then a warning will be required unless the danger is one of general knowledge (as probably is the case with the danger of trichinae in raw pork). The last sentence of the comment indicates that it applies only to known dangers. But the reference to "new or experimental drugs" earlier in the comment suggests that it applies to unknowable dangers as well, and the *Toner* court so held.

The reason to distinguish between unknown, and known but unpreventable, risks, is that a warning of known risks may enable the user to avoid the danger if she has a reasonable choice of how or whether or not to use the product. The effect of a warning may be minimal, however, if, as in Gaston v. Hunter (1978), the court concludes that the warning need only state that the drug or product is experimental when specific dangers are unknown. Such a warning is little more than a disclaimer of liability.

If the comment applies to all unknowable manufacturing or production (that is, random) defects, as well as to defects in design, then it may eliminate any distinction between production and design defects as far as strict liability is concerned. It makes liability turn upon the ability to know in both instances, while strict liability is imposed even though "the seller has exercised all possible care in the preparation and sale of his product." Rest. 2d of Torts § 402A. If knowability is eliminated for purposes of comment *k*, then unavoidably unsafe and state of the art may be the same defense.

In Brown v. Superior Court (1988), the court held that strict liability does not apply in the case of misrepresentation where the product is unavoidably unsafe. This holding is out of line with the general rule imposing strict liability for misrepresentation that causes personal injury.

The failure, even of an expert, to discover that which is knowable is not necessarily the same as the failure to exercise reasonable care, since something can be knowable but not reasonably discoverable. If such a distinction is made, then liability under comment *k* may be stricter than that of negligence, but not completely strict in the sense in which knowability as well as reason to know as of the date of manufacture would be irrelevant to liability.

For known but unpreventable defects, the comment may merely embody the standard of ordinary consumer expectations. If the danger of the hepatitis virus in blood is known, the ordinary consumer may prefer to take the risk of hepatitis rather than the greater one of dying from lack of blood. Application of the consumer expectation standard is more problematical where the danger is unknown. It is very doubtful, for example, that many or any mothers would have taken diethylstilbestrol (DES) as an antiabortifacient if they had known that the drug was ineffective and a carcinogen as well. The ordinary consumer did not consciously take these risks by ingesting the drug, since she did not contemplate the danger. But if one assumes knowledge of danger, on the part of either the consumer or the seller, then it would be unreasonable to sell the carcinogen. Moreover, if the date of trial is used as the time for determining knowledge, then consumer expectations as of that time can readily supply the standard for determining defectiveness.

Even if comment *k* applies to unknowable production (random) defects, it still may not apply to all products. The court in Wilkinson v. Bay Shore Lumber Co. (1986) held that defendant failed to show it applied to lumber with concealed dry rot, and "the few reported decisions in this jurisdiction which refer to comment *k* overwhelmingly involve products such as prescription drugs, vaccines, blood, and medical devices such as intrauterine devices and breast implants." The court in Collins v. Eli Lilly Co. (1984) held that the comment would not even apply to the drug DES, since that drug was not new or experimental when marketed in view of the long period available for testing.

Other courts have not been so restrictive in their interpretation. The Fifth Circuit in Borel v. Fibreboard Paper Products Corp. (1973) assumed the comment applied to asbestos products; the Seventh Circuit in Filler v. Rayex Corp. (1970) assumed it applied to sunglasses; and the Tennessee Court of Appeals in Carr v. International Harvester (1979) (rotary mower) indicated that the comment applied to products in general. The court in Purvis v. PPG Industries, Inc. (1987) applied the comment to a dry cleaning solvent with a known danger that had been warned against, and noted that the comment had been applied in other cases to a surgical drape, asbestos insulation, blood, and an intrauterine device.

The courts have divided over whether comment k should apply to bar strict liability across the board in the case of prescription drugs, or whether the determination if a product is unavoidably unsafe (i.e., whether its utility outweighs its risk) should be made on a case by case basis. Grundberg v. Upjohn Co. (1991) stands for the proposition that an across the board rule should be applied to all FDA-approved prescription drugs. Savina v. Sterling Drug, Inc. (1990) and West v. Searle & Co. (1991) adopt a case by case approach. The court in Shanks v. Upjohn Co. (1992) adopted a risk-benefit analysis which is the same as a case by case approach. In Hill v. Searle Laboratories (1989) the court adopted a case by case approach to deny comment k immunity for the CU–7 intrauterine device. It found that there were alternative birth control measures available, that the CU–7 was not "exceptionally beneficial to society", and that the defendant, "through mass advertising and merchandising practices, generated a general sense of product quality, making it difficult for consumers to fully understand the risks involved with the use of an IUD."

The Restatement of course is not law, but it has had great influence on the courts in their attempts to arrive at the law by common law development. If comment *k* is applied to all reasonably unknowable defects of production as well as of design, then strict liability is effectively excluded from the law of products liability except for cases of actionable innocent misrepresentation or abnormally dangerous activities. An action in negligence would remain, but negligence could not be established for defects that were not reasonably knowable.

Comment *k* could be restricted to the category of medical products, but the justification for doing so is not clear and the parameters of the category could not be readily defined. Of course the three factors of production defect, unknowable dangers, and products in general may not be applied to comment *k* cases by all courts, and some courts may limit the application of one or more of these factors when applying the comment. Also, a court may apply the language of § 402A (liability for a defective product even though the seller "has exercised all possible care") and disregard the conflicting language in comment *k* to that section.

## 4. DEFECT AND UNREASONABLE DANGER

Section 402A of the Second Restatement of Torts states that one who sells any product "in a defective condition unreasonably dangerous" can be held strictly liable for injuries resulting from the use or consumption of the product. Most courts follow the language of § 402A in applying strict tort liability and thus require proof that the product is "in a defective condition" and "unreasonably dangerous", although the category of plaintiffs has generally been extended to include foreseeable bystanders as well as users and consumers.

Several courts have indicated that the terms "defective condition" and "unreasonable danger" are synonymous, see Burks v. Firestone Tire & Rubber Co. (1981), Bowman v. General Motors Corp. (1977), and the comments to § 402A support this conclusion. Comment *g* defines a "defective condition" as one "not contemplated by the ultimate consumer, which will be unreasonably dangerous to him." Comment *i* defines "unreasonably dangerous" as "dangerous to an extent beyond that which would be contemplated by the ordinary consumer who purchases it, with the ordinary knowledge common to the community as to its characteristics." One definition defines consumer expectations regarding defectiveness in terms of unreasonable danger, and the other defines unreasonable danger in terms of ordinary consumer expectations.

A few courts, notably California in Cronin v. J.B.E. Olson Corp. (1972), have refused to charge "unreasonable danger" on the grounds that it "rings of negligence." In Barker v. Lull Engineering Co., Inc. (1978), the court defined defect alternatively in terms of ordinary consumer expectations and risk-benefit balancing, giving the plaintiff the option of proceeding on either theory. The court recognized that risk-benefit balancing is a reasonableness test that "introduces an element which 'rings of negligence' into the determination of defect." It stated that its concern in *Cronin,* however, was that the term "unreasonably dangerous ... burdened *the injured plaintiff* with proof of an element that rings of negligence," and that this concern could be met by shifting the burden of proof to the defendant on the risk-benefit issue.

## 5. THE RELATION OF DEFECT TO CAUSES OF ACTION

As can be seen from the preceding discussion, courts have attempted to identify the types of things that can be considered actionably wrong with a product. These have generally been identified as four: 1) production defects, 2) design defects, 3) inadequate warnings, and 4) misrepresentations. The courts have then undertaken to define these types of defects and this effort implicates the causes of action discussed in the next chapter. Misrepresentation is *sui generis,* since it is usually recognized as giving rise to an action for both culpable and innocent misrepresentation—the former in tort, and the latter in both tort and warranty. With regard to the other types of defect (production, design, and warning), the law of products liability presents considerable uncertainty regarding the relationship of fault and strict liability.

It seems fair to conclude that the risk-benefit approach looks toward fault, while the consumer expectation test (whether used in implied warranty or tort) looks toward strict liability. Except in the case of production defects that do not involve unavoidably unsafe products, and innocent misrepresentation, the courts have had difficulty in working out a doctrine of strict products liability significantly different from fault liability. Even a finding that a product should not have been marketed at all, regardless of whether it could have been made safer, suggests fault on the part of the marketer in putting the product on the market in the first place.

It is possible that products law will in the future shift more toward a causation approach, exemplified by the strict tort doctrine of abnormally dangerous activities. Alternatively, it may become avowedly fault-oriented, even with regard to production defects and misrepresentation. With regard to the latter basis of recovery, first amendment freedom of speech considerations may dictate a shift to a fault analysis.

## C.  WHAT IS A SALE?

It is traditionally said that products liability law applies to the sale of defective products. A "sale" is defined in the Unif. Comm. Code as "the pass-

ing of title from the seller to the buyer for a price."
UCC § 2–106(1). The courts, however, have not
generally insisted on a technical finding of passage
of title before products liability law is applied. If
the sale is not by one in the regular course of
business of selling the product, then strict liability
normally does not apply unless the seller makes an
express warranty or a warranty of fitness for a
particular purpose. The sale usually need not be
to the plaintiff, as long as the defendant has sold to
someone and the plaintiff is a foreseeable claimant—except that privity of contract may be retained for warranty actions in some jurisdictions,
particularly with regard to claims involving only
economic loss.

Strict liability for the supply of products has
been extended to the builder-vendor of houses, Mc-
Donald v. Mianecki (1979), and to product leases,
Cintrone v. Hertz Truck Leasing & Rental Service
(1965). It has been applied to products made available to facilitate the sale of another product, Shaf-
fer v. Victoria Station, Inc. (1978) (wine glass); to
products offered for sale, Delaney v. Towmotor
Corp. (1964) (forklift truck made available on a try-
out basis); to hotel premises, Becker v. IRM Corp.
(1985); and to professional services, Gentile v.
MacGregor Mfg. Co. (1985).

The issue of the scope of transactions covered by
products liability is relevant primarily for purposes
of determining the extent of implied strict products
liability, since all other transactions are usually

subject to the law of negligence unless there is some applicable immunity. It may be that the law of strict liability will eventually be extended to all business providers of products, realty, and services. The law of products liability has generally been an expanding subject, with the expansion implemented by policy considerations of providing a safer environment and compensation to the injured, and by the unwillingness of the courts to draw technical distinctions between similar categories of activity. The rationale for not applying implied strict liability to the occasional supplier of goods, realty or services is that such a supplier is not an expert with regard to the commodity supplied and is often in no better position than the claimant to prevent injury or spread the risk of loss. The person who occasionally engages in abnormally dangerous activities, however, may be strictly liable, for here the rationale may be that one who engages in such an activity assumes the risk of the consequences. Likewise, the person who occasionally expressly warrants his goods or services can be held strictly liable because of the justifiable reliance on such representations.

A majority of jurisdictions provide by statute that the furnishing of blood and blood products is not a sale but a service to which the implied warranties do not apply, and these statutes have widely been construed to prohibit the imposition of strict tort liability as well. Zichichi v. Middlesex Mem. Hosp. (1987). The *Zichichi* court recognized that an action for negligence in the supply of blood is not precluded by such statutes, and presumably an action for misrepresentation would also lie—in any situation where either negligence or misrepresentation on the part of the defendant supplier could be shown.

# CHAPTER II

# THE CAUSES OF ACTION AND DAMAGES

## A. HISTORICAL EVOLUTION—THE BREAKDOWN OF PRIVITY

The English court in Winterbottom v. Wright (1842) held that a mailcoachman did not state a cause of action against the defendant, who had contracted with plaintiff's employer to maintain plaintiff's mailcoach in proper repair. Plaintiff was injured when the mailcoach broke down as he was driving it, the accident occurring because of defendant's allegedly negligent failure to perform the contract of repair.

In denying recovery, Baron Alderson said: "The only safe rule is to confine the right to recover to those who enter into the contract: if we go one step beyond that, there is no reason why we should not go fifty." Baron Rolfe, concurring in the judgment, noted that the only breach of duty alleged in the complaint was defendant's "omission to keep the carriage in a safe condition," not affirmative negligent repair. He presumably would have decided the case on the then well-recognized distinction between negligent acts and negligent omissions to perform a contractual duty, there being no duty to third persons to perform a contractual obligation. The case was not thus limited in later decisions, however, and it became generally interpreted as precedent relieving a contractual party from liability in negligence to persons not a party to the contract, whether the contractual party was guilty of misperformance or nonperformance.

*Winterbottom* was followed in this country for approximately three quarters of a century. An exception was early made for negligently mislabeled products, Thomas v. Winchester (1852), and then for negligently made products that were considered "imminently dangerous", Loop v. Litchfield (1870) (defective balance wheel on circular saw). The "imminently dangerous" exception was not readily definable, and eventually the exception swallowed the rule in MacPherson v. Buick Motor Co. (1916) (rotten wooden spokes in car wheel).

In *MacPherson* Judge Cardozo, speaking for the New York Court of Appeals, said the category of imminently dangerous products "is not limited to poisons, explosives, and things of like nature, to things which in their normal operation are implements of destruction. If the nature of a thing is such that it is reasonably certain to place life and limb in peril when negligently made, it is then a thing of danger.... Precedents drawn from the days of travel by stage coach do not fit the conditions of travel today. The principle that the danger must be imminent does not change, but the things subject to the principle do change." *Mac-*

*Pherson* was soon widely adopted as the general rule in America. It likewise applies to actions for fraud and recklessness.

The privity requirement in warranty met a similar fate in this country. Privity was early dispensed with in express warranty cases, as in Baxter v. Ford Motor Co. (1932). An exception was also made in implied warranty for dangerous foodstuffs, Mazetti v. Armour & Co. (1913), and for articles of intimate body use such as cosmetics, Rogers v. Toni Home Permanent Co. (1958). Then in Henningsen v. Bloomfield Motors, Inc. (1960), the New Jersey Supreme Court in a defective car case abolished the privity requirement for implied warranty cases generally. Said Justice Francis, speaking for the court: "We see no rational doctrinal basis for differentiating between a fly in a bottle of beverage and a defective automobile." *Henningsen,* like *MacPherson* before it, was soon widely followed in the United States.

Strict tort products liability evolved in large part to avoid the privity requirement and other restrictions of warranty law, such as notice of breach, disclaimer and the warranty statute of limitations. The rationale for strict tort is set forth in Greenman v. Yuba Power Products, Inc. (1963), which has also been generally followed in this country. This rationale will be discussed below in the section on strict liability.

The breakdown of the privity requirement is one of the hallmarks of modern products liability.

This occurrence is a classic example of the evolutionary nature of the common law, as it develops to meet the felt necessities of the time.

## B. NEGLIGENCE

Negligence can arise in numerous ways—through inadequate inspection, processing, packaging, warning, design, marketing, or in any way in which a defendant fails to meet the standard of care of a reasonable person in dealing with a product thereby proximately causing injury to the plaintiff. Negligent handling of a product can result in a product defect, such as a production or design flaw. But there may be nothing wrong with the product itself, although the defendant can owe a duty of care as for example when it negligently entrusts a product to a minor, Moning v. Alfono (1977) (slingshot), or to one who apparently does not recognize an inherent danger in the product, Ray v. Suburban Supply Co. (1982) (supply of wet cement to workers who did not recognize the danger of skin contact with the product). The latter situation resembles an ordinary case of failure to warn, except here the duty to warn may be owed to a special group and not to the public at large.

The Supreme Court of Arkansas, in Elk Corp. of Arkansas v. Jackson (1987), held that a manufacturer who dangerously double-stacked felt roofing rolls on a flatbed trailer for hauling by plaintiff could be liable only in negligence, and not in strict liability, for resulting injuries to the plaintiff when the load shifted causing plaintiff's truck to overturn. "If Elk was at fault, then it was because Elk negligently loaded Jackson's trailer, not because the rolls of roofing were defective."

The *Jackson* court denied plaintiff's petition to rehear, wherein plaintiff pointed out his contention that the roofing bundles were defective not just because of double-stacking, but also because the bundles were held together by only one rather than by two metal bands. The court unpersuasively attempted to distinguish Stalter v. Coca–Cola Bottling Co. of Arkansas (1984), where it had held that a bottle carton was a defective product because the carton "was obviously intended to be an integral part of the product and its use", while the bands here were "simply to secure the load for shipping." It then stated that the double-stacking and banding "all contributed to making the load dangerous", and that plaintiff "should not be allowed to single out one step in that process which can be loosely described as packaging", in order to assert strict liability and avoid the burden of proving negligence. This case well demonstrates the occasional difficulty of distinguishing an ordinary negligence case from a strict products liability suit.

A duty of care in one's relation to a product can exist not just in connection with the sale or supply of the product. It can also arise in connection with product repair, whether or not the repairer is the seller.

The duty of care can be breached if one negligently misrepresents a product, either at the time of sale or at any other time. For example, if a seller represents that his product has a safety feature, without having reason to believe that it does, he may be liable in negligent misrepresentation for resulting damages. Cunningham v. C. R. Pease (1908) (stove blacking). If he by assertion pretends to know something that in fact he does not know, he can be liable for negligent misrepresentation. Pabon v. Hackensack Auto Sales, Inc. (1960) (dealer told buyer not to worry about noise in steering of new car, that the noise was typical of new cars and would "wear out").

A person can be guilty of negligence in relation to a product whether or not he or she is in the regular business of selling such a product. The duty of care owed by a business seller or other professional is often higher than that owed by a lay person, however, with the professional being held to the standard of an expert regarding the goods.

Many states have enacted special products liability statutes that generally retrench on the rights of plaintiffs to bring a products action. These statutes may not apply to an action in which the defendant is sued for negligence other than in his capacity as a product supplier. In the non-sales context, a product-related negligence action may be no different from any other negligence suit.

The federal Third Circuit in Repola v. Morbark Industries, Inc. (1991) held that the New Jersey products liability statute applied to a claim for failure to warn, even though the failure arose out of an alleged agreement separate from the sales contract. Therefore, the cou:t said, the plaintiff was not entitled to a separate jury instruction based on common law negligence.

Some state products liability statutes are limited to wrongful death, personal injury and property damage claims. See, e.g., Tenn. Code Ann. § 29–28–102(6). Such statutes arguably do not apply to claims for pure economic loss, whether brought in negligence or strict liability.

The doctrine of res ipsa loquitur can apply to products liability suits, as well as to negligence suits in general. Here the plaintiff must show that the accident is of a kind that ordinarily does not occur in the absence of negligence, that responsible causes other than the defendant are sufficiently eliminated by the evidence, and that the indicated negligence is within the scope of the defendant's duty to the plaintiff. Rest. 2d of Torts § 328D.

Thus the explosion of a soda pop bottle that was not mishandled after it left the defendant's hands gave rise to an inference of negligence in Escola v. Coca Cola Bottling Co. of Fresno (1944), even though no specific act of negligence on the defendant's part could be shown. Similarly, res ipsa was applied in McGonigal v. Gearhart Industries, Inc. (1986) to the premature explosion of a grenade allegedly caused by a missing delay fuse whose absence plaintiffs contended could have been detected by careful x-ray inspections conducted by defendant in the manufacturing process. Res ipsa applied although plaintiffs "were unable to introduce direct evidence" of defendant's negligence "because the x-rays of the defective grenade were destroyed in the normal course of business." Indeed, many courts hold that if the plaintiff pleads or proves specific acts of negligence, the doctrine of res ipsa loquitur cannot be applied.

## C.  STATUTORY VIOLATIONS

The violation of a penal statute can give rise to negligence per se, if the plaintiff is within the class of persons protected by the statute and the risk involved is within the statute's coverage. Thus, mislabeling a product in violation of the federal Food, Drug and Cosmetic Act was held negligence per se in Orthopedic Equip. Co. v. Eutsler (1960). Such a statutory violation may be considered as merely evidence of negligence or an unexcused violation may be treated as conclusive on the negligence issue. Lowe v. General Motors Corp. (1980) (violation of Nat. Traffic and Motor Vehicle Safety Act). Where the violation is treated as conclusive, negligence per se is like strict liability.

In addition, a cause of action may be expressly or impliedly created by a statute or regulation, whether the statute be civil or penal in nature. The form of the cause of action, which can be for strict liability, negligence or wilfulness, depends on the terms of the statute or the intent of the legislative or regulatory body.

Thus, an action for breach of implied or express warranty is explicitly created by the Uniform Commercial Code—although courts may also create a parallel common law cause of action for breach of warranty. For example, a warranty of habitability usually arises by common law, rather than by statute. Violation of state consumer protection statutes can give rise to a cause of action, often for treble damages. An action for recission of the purchase of a defective automobile can arise under state "lemon laws." If it can be shown that a manufacturer knew of a product problem, and attempted by a pattern of criminal conduct to conceal the problem, the manufacturer may be civilly liable for treble damages and attorneys fees under the Racketeer Influenced and Corrupt Organizations Act (RICO), 18 U.S.C. § 1961 et seq. (1984).

In Swenson v. Emerson Elec. Co. (1985), the court held that a private cause of action could be implied under the federal Consumer Product Safety Act, since it found that Congress intended to provide "simply another source of liability in addition to the typical claims which arise from injuries caused by consumer products: negligence, breach of warranty, and strict liability." While a manufacturer was not liable in negligence, strict tort or implied warranty for marketing lawn darts, which were obviously dangerous, it could be found guilty, said the court in First Nat. Bank of Dwight v. Regent Sports Corp. (1986), for violating Consumer Product Safety Commission regulations that prohibit the knowing marketing of such darts to children.

The court held in Minichello v. U.S. Industries, Inc. (1985) that evidence of compliance or noncompliance with OSHA regulations should not be admissible in a products liability action against a manufacturer. The court reached this conclusion for two reasons. First, the Act expressly states that it is not intended to enlarge, diminish, or affect in any way the common law rights of injured employees. Second, "OSHA regulations pertain only to employers' conduct," and they do not set standards for manufacturers of workplace machinery. In Bunn v. Caterpillar Tractor Co. (1976), on the other hand, the court held that OSHA regulations were admissible against the manufacturer of workplace machinery to determine if the machine was unreasonably dangerous, provided the jury was "properly instructed ... that the Regulations were *not* to be considered as binding upon the Defendant."

## D. RECKLESS MISCONDUCT, CONCEALMENT AND DECEIT

One of the most publicized cases in which the defendant was held liable for reckless misconduct is Grimshaw v. Ford Motor Co. (1981). This case was one of many against Ford for its placement of the Pinto gas tank so that fires entering the passenger compartment were frequent after rear-end collisions. Allegedly the positioning of the tank and failure to secure it against fires were knowingly done by Ford as part of its effort to produce an economy car. A punitive damage award of $125 million, remitted to $3½ million, was sustained by the California Court of Appeal.

A case combining reckless misconduct, concealment and deceit is Gillham v. Admiral Corp. (1975). There the defendant was found guilty of recklessness in using unsuitable paper and wax materials as insulation in the high voltage transformers of its television sets. Superior materials were available, and used by other television manufacturers. Defendant's own testing revealed that its sets were prone to catch fire because of the inadequate insulation. Defendant received a steady stream of complaints about fires originating in its color television sets, and by the time of plaintiff's injury "at least 91 such fires had been reported to Admiral." Yet defendant made no effort to redesign its set, or to inform purchasers and prospective purchasers of the hazard. On the contrary, defendant "misled customers by informing them that the sets were safe." It was held liable in compensatory and punitive damages for fire injuries to plaintiff resulting from such a defective set.

Intentional misrepresentations can counteract what might otherwise be adequate warnings of danger.  In Johnson v. Colt Industries Operating Corp. (1986), the defendant was held liable for compensatory and punitive damages in marketing a .22 revolver that could discharge if there were a cartridge in the chamber under the hammer when the hammer was accidentally struck.  A statement in the instructions accompanying the gun said "the safest way to carry your [gun] is with five cartridges in the chamber and the hammer on the sixth chamber," but this statement was counteracted by others indicating that the gun could be fully loaded safely.

A punitive damage judgment of $7½ million was awarded in Sterling v. Velsicol Chem. Corp. (1986), for defendant's reckless burial of ultrahazardous chemical wastes on a landsite adjoining plaintiffs' property in violation of state law, with resulting contamination of the surrounding aquifer.  The case was tried on theories of abnormal danger, negligence, trespass and nuisance.  It does not fit the usual category of products liability suits, since defendant neither sold the chemical wastes nor held them out for sale.  However, defendant did sell products of which the wastes were a byproduct. The wastes could therefore be viewed as defective products that were incidental to the sale of other products—such as a defective shopping cart used in a grocery store, for which strict products liability can be imposed.  Alternatively, abnormally dangerous activities involving dangerous products can be viewed as within the scope of the developing law of products liability.

Reckless misconduct can justify recovery of damages for solely emotional distress, which would not otherwise be recoverable. In Wisniewski v. Johns–Manville Corp. (1987), the court stated that plaintiffs would be able to recover for emotional distress resulting from fear of contracting cancer as a result of exposure to their husbands' or fathers' work clothes containing asbestos dust. They had failed to show intentional or reckless misconduct on the part of the defendants, however, so such recovery was denied on the facts of the case. Moreover, plaintiffs failed to show that their fears of contracting asbestos-related illnesses were the "natural and probable consequences of defendants' failure to place warning labels on their finished asbestos products."

A plaintiff may be able to recover in fraud where an action for negligence or strict liability will not lie. Learjet v. Spenlinhauer (1990) (no recovery in negligent misrepresentation without privity for pure economic loss, but recovery allowed for fraudulent misrepresentation); Kahn v. Shiley Inc. (1990) (recovery in fraudulent misrepresentation, but not in strict liability, for emotional distress caused by defective heart valve.)

The mere fact that defendant has been sued numerous times regarding an alleged defective product does not prove wilful or wanton misconduct, absent proof of the nature and disposition of the other suits. Evidence that 31 lawsuits had been brought against a ladder manufacturer was held insufficient to show recklessness in Keller Industries, Inc. v. Waters (1987), where the plaintiff was able to identify only one such case that resulted in judgment against the defendant.

## E.  STRICT LIABILITY
### 1.  IN GENERAL

Hallmarks of the modern law of products liability are the elimination of the privity requirement in an action against the seller of a defective product, discussed at the beginning of this chapter, and the development of the doctrine of strict liability. Strict liability for breach of warranty is a remedy dating back at least to the Middle Ages, but the full development of strict products liability awaited the elimination of the privity requirement in the 20th century.

Strict liability in tort had its modern origins in warranty, and in the tort doctrine of res ipsa loquitur. See Escola v. Coca Cola Bottling Co. of Fresno (1944). Also, the tort doctrine of strict liability for abnormally dangerous activities may account in a significant way for the development of strict tort liability for defective products. See Chapman Chem. Co. v. Taylor ( 1949). Comment *n* to the strict products liability § 402A of Rest. 2d of Torts adopts the rule regarding contributory negligence that is applied to strict liability for abnormally dangerous activities, as set forth in Rest. 2d of Torts § 524, thus indicating the influence of one doctrine on the other.

The rationales for imposing strict liability are perhaps best set forth by Justice Traynor in his concurrence in the *Escola* case: The manufacturer is in the best position to reduce the risk; the loss may be overwhelming to the injured person, but it can be effectively insured against by the manufacturer and distributed among the public as a cost of doing business; the manufacturer, even if not negligent, is responsible for the product being on the market; in leaving problematical cases to the jury, the negligence rule often approaches that of strict liability; the strict liability rule of pure food statutes provides a persuasive example by analogy; the buyer can sue in strict liability for breach of warranty against the retailer, who has an action over against his own seller and so on up the chain of distribution, so the original action should be allowed against the manufacturer in strict liability without privity to avoid needless circuity of actions; the consumer lacks the means and skill to investigate the soundness of a product for herself, and her vigilance has been lulled by manufacturer advertising and market devices such as trademarks. Twenty years later, in Greenman v. Yuba Power Products, Inc. (1963), Justice Traynor speaking for the majority added yet another reason for strict liability: the product by its appearance belies "the defect lurking beneath the surface", and the buyer assumes that it will "safely do the jobs it was built to do."

As noted in the first chapter, courts are ambivalent about applying strict liability to warning and design cases, and to cases involving unavoidably unsafe products. Where stric. liability *is* implied, it is normally only against a business provider. However, strict liability is regularly applied in both tort and warranty against business persons for misrepresentation, and the nonbusiness person can also be strictly liable for breach of express warranty. Moreover, strict liability for engaging in abnormally dangerous activities is imposed against business and nonbusiness persons alike, even where the activity involves the use of a non-defective product.

## 2. IMPLIED OBLIGATIONS

### a. The Warranty of Merchantability

Section 2–314 of the Uniform Commercial Code provides:

(1) Unless excluded or modified (Section 2–316), a warranty that the goods shall be merchantable is implied in a contract for their sale if the seller is a merchant with respect to goods of that kind. Under this section the serving for value of food or drink to be consumed either on the premises or elsewhere is a sale.

(2) Goods to be merchantable must be at least such as

(a) pass without objection in the trade under the contract description; and

(b) in the case of fungible goods, are of fair average quality within the description; and

(c) are fit for the ordinary purposes for which such goods are used; and

(d) run, within the variations permitted by the agreement, of even kind, quality and quantity within each unit and among all units involved; and

(e) are adequately contained, packaged, and labeled as the agreement may require; and

(f) conform to the promises or affirmations of fact made on the container or label if any.

(3) Unless excluded or modified (Section 2–316) other implied warranties may arise from course of dealing or usage of trade.

The Sales Article (Article Two, of which the implied and express warranties are a part) has been adopted in all states except Louisiana, and by the District of Columbia and the Virgin Islands.

The implied warranty of merchantability arises only when the seller is a merchant, defined in UCC § 2–104(1) as "a person who deals in goods of the kind" or otherwise by his occupation or by the employment of an agent or broker or other intermediary "holds himself out as having knowledge or skill peculiar to the practices or goods involved."

The Code does not expressly require privity of contract, and comment 2 to § 2–313 states that "warranties need not be confined either to sales contracts or to the direct parties to such a contract." Some courts, however, continue to impose the privity requirement in an action for breach of warranty, e.g., Miller v. Sears, Roebuck & Co. (1986). Section 2–318 abolishes the privity requirement for certain persons associated with the buyer, depending on which version of the section is adopted. Some states have abolished privity by statute, e.g., Tenn. Code Ann. § 29–34–104, and many more have done so by common law development, at least where physical injury to person or property is involved. As will be seen in Chapter IV, the privity requirement is widely retained in actions for solely economic loss, and the plaintiff is often restricted to an action in warranty in such cases.

UCC § 2–316 provides that implied warranties may be excluded or modified, and § 2–719 provides that remedies for breach of warranty may be modified or limited. The scope of these sections will be considered in Chapter IV.

Most states provide by statute that there are no implied warranties in the sale of blood, blood products, or human tissues, e.g., Tenn. Code Ann. § 47–2–316(5). Such statutes, or the policies behind them (akin to the "unavoidably-unsafe-product" rationale considered in Chapter I), have also been held to prohibit an action in implied strict tort liability. These rules do not prohibit an action for recklessness or negligence, or for reckless, negligent or innocent misrepresentation, if such can be proven.

Section 2–314 is not intended to exhaust the description of the implied warranty of merchantability. Goods to be merchantable must be "at least" such as are described in § 2–314(2), the key provision thereof being subsec. (c) ("fit for the ordinary purposes for which such goods are used"). Subsec. (3) states that "other implied warranties may arise from course of dealing or usage of trade", and presumably from other sources as well such as implied understandings and the like.

### b. The Warranty of Fitness for a Particular Purpose

UCC § 2–315 provides:

Where the seller at the time of contracting has reason to know any particular purpose for which the goods are required and that the buyer is relying on the seller's skill or judgment to select or furnish suitable goods, there is unless excluded or modified under the next section an implied warranty that the goods shall be fit for such purpose.

This warranty is often treated interchangeably with the implied warranty of merchantability, but the two are not the same. The seller here need not be a merchant, and buyer reliance is required.

These distinctions are not ironclad, however. For example, in Hebron Pub. School v. U.S. Gypsum Co. (1992) the court held that the plaintiff was not required to prove reliance to recover on the warranty of fitness, since the plaintiff's claim was "grounded in tort [and] not in contract." And comment 4 to UCC § 2–315 says that while the fitness warranty "can arise as to nonmerchants where this is justified by the circumstances," nevertheless the warranty will "normally" arise "only where the seller is a merchant with the appropriate 'skill or judgment.'"

A particular purpose may be different from the general purpose of merchantability. As the court said in Ingram River Equip., Inc. v. Pott Indus., Inc. (1987), "the key inquiry is not whether anyone else can be found who put the goods to the same use, but whether the buyer's use is sufficiently different from the customary use of the goods to make it not an ordinary use of goods; that a buyer's use is not entirely idiosyncratic does not mean that it is ordinary." The court found that steam coil systems, purchased "to carry petroleum products on the Mississippi and its tributaries and to heat those products to facilitate their discharge in cold climates," were products purchased for a particular purpose.

The fitness warranty is one of strict liability (although negligence may of course also be present), since the seller's selection or furnishing of the goods, and his knowledge of the buyer's reliance on his skill or judgment, may be entirely reasonable. The "particular purpose" nature of the warranty causes it to resemble the express warranty, so that strict liability may be imposed here even though it would not otherwise be implied in merchantability or strict tort.

The warranty is of fitness "at the time of contracting." Since many courts hold that an express warranty can arise in a post-sale context, annot., 47 ALR 4th 200 (1986), the fitness warranty conceivably can also arise after the contract is made. This conclusion is supported by UCC § 2–209(1), which provides that "[a]n agreement modifying a contract within this Article needs no consideration to be binding."

### c. Strict Tort Products Liability

Section 402A of the Rest. 2d of Torts states:

(1) One who sells any product in a defective condition unreasonably dangerous to the user or consumer or to his property is subject to liability for physical harm thereby caused to the ultimate user or consumer, or to his property, if

(a) the seller is engaged in the business of selling such a product, and

(b) it is expected to and does reach the user or consumer without substantial change in the condition in which it is sold.

(2) The rule stated in Subsection (1) applies although

(a) the seller has exercised all possible care in the preparation and sale of his product, and

(b) the user or consumer has not bought the product from or entered into any contractual relation with the seller.

This section has been widely adopted as the common law or statutory rule in the overwhelming majority of American jurisdictions. Ogle v. Caterpillar Tractor Co. (1986).

The section evolved as a consumer remedy to escape the warranty restrictions such as privity, notice of breach, disclaimers and limitations of remedies. It applies to a seller "engaged in the business" of selling a product—essentially the same person as a merchant seller described in the warranty of merchantability. The limitation of claimants to users and consumers has widely been disregarded, and any foreseeable plaintiff is typically allowed to sue. Recovery, however, is often limited to damages for physical harm to person or property resulting from a product supplied in a defective condition that is unreasonably dangerous. The meaning of "defect" is examined in Chapter I, and the meaning of "physical harm" is considered in Chapter IV.

As noted in the first chapter, many courts are reluctant to impose strict liability in design or warning cases, or in cases where the product is considered unavoidably unsafe or in compliance with the state of the art when made. A true strict liability approach, however, is represented by cases such as Habecker v. Clark Equip. Co. (1991). There the court said that evidence of computer modeling capabilities (state of the art) in existence when defendant's forklift was manufactured was inadmissible. "This rule can be justified because it provides manufacturers with an incentive to invest, not only in proven safety features, but also in the testing and development of any new feature that may prove superior."

### d. Abnormal Danger

Section 519 of the Rest. 2d of Torts states that "[o]ne who carries on an abnormally dangerous activity is subject to liability for harm to the person, land or chattels of another resulting from the activity, although he has exercised the utmost care to prevent the harm." The abnormal danger doctrine originated with the liability for non-natural use of land, as that doctrine was developed in Rylands v. Fletcher [1868], and came to be known in this country under the rubric of "ultrahazardous activity." The Rest. 2d of Torts adopted the term "abnormally dangerous activity."

Section 520 of the Rest. 2d of Torts sets forth the factors which are considered in determining whether an activity is ultrahazardous or abnormally dangerous. They are: a) the existence of a high degree of risk, b) the likelihood that the harm will be great, c) the inability to eliminate the risk by the exercise of reasonable care, d) the extent to which the activity is not a matter of common usage, e) the inappropriateness of the activity to the place where it is carried on, and f) the extent to which its value to the community is outweighed by its dangerous attributes. Comment *f* to this section states that ordinarily several of these factors will be required for strict liability, but that "it is not necessary that each of them be present, especially if others weigh heavily." The doctrine has been applied, for example, to an activity that is appropriate and valuable to the community, Cities Service Co. v. State (1975) (phosphate slime pond), and to an activity where the risk could be eliminated by the exercise of reasonable care, Clark–Aiken Co. v. Cromwell–Wright Co., Inc. (1975) (water escape from failure of dam).

The trial court in Indiana Harbor Belt R. Co. v. American Cyanamid Co. (1981) held that the manufacturer and shipper of a flammable, toxic liquid called acrylonitrile could be held strictly liable for damages resulting from an abnormally dangerous activity, where the liquid escaped from the tank car in which it was being shipped. The court of appeals reversed (1990), in large part on the questionable ground that negligence was likely present in the maintenance of the tank car, so that liability for an abnormally dangerous activity did not apply. As noted above, courts and the Restatement recognize that strict liability for an abnormally dangerous activity can apply even though negligence is present.

The plaintiff in *Indiana Harbor* apparently did not argue strict products liability, although this doctrine would seem to have applied. The product container (the tank car) was defective, and most courts recognize that strict products liability applies where either the product or its container is defective. Moreover, the likely presence of negligence normally does not bar a strict products liability claim.

Courts have held that strict liability for products is separate and distinct from that for abnormally dangerous activities. For example, in a case in which the applicable statute of limitations was at issue, the court in Cavan v. General Motors Corp. (1977) said that the rule of *Rylands v. Fletcher* "is applied when an *activity* creates an abnormally dangerous condition, or by its nature presents extraordinary risk of harm to person or property." The fact that a product "may create an 'ultrahazardous condition' by virtue of defective design or manufacture is . . . of no moment under our present law."

A number of suits have been brought alleging strict tort liability under Rest. 2d of Torts §§ 402A and 519 (products liability and abnormally dangerous activity) for the manufacture and sale of handguns. All of them have been dismissed except one, Kelley v. R.G. Industries, Inc. (1985).

The *Kelley* court, like many other courts, held that the manufacture and sale of handguns is not a "land-related" activity so as to invoke the abnormal danger doctrine. This holding is questionable, since many of the abnormal danger cases are not land-related. See, e.g., Siegler v. Kuhlman (1972) (spillage of gasoline from gasoline truck onto public highway). The court also said that the doctrine only applied to the use of a product, not to its manufacture—a proximate cause analysis.

The court found the gun met consumer expectations in products liability because the ordinary consumer "would expect a handgun to be dangerous." The gun also met the risk-utility test because "[t]his standard is only applied when something goes wrong with the product."

The court then fashioned a new test—which resembles the social utility test discussed in the section on defects in the first chapter—wherein the fact finder could impose liability if it found that the handgun involved was a "so-called Saturday Night Special, which is considered to have little or no legitimate purpose in today's society." The characteristics of this gun—its small size, short barrel, low cost, poor quality, and unreliability—make it "particularly attractive for criminal use and virtually useless for the legitimate purposes of law enforcement, sport, and protection of persons, property and businesses."

Many courts have refused to impose strict liability on handgun manufacturers because they think this is an appropriate subject for legislative determination in view of the fact that the manufacture and possession of handguns are legal and approved activities. See, e.g., Martin v. Harrington & Richardson, Inc. (1984). Indeed, California and Idaho have by statute forbidden a products liability determination that guns or ammunition is defectively designed because the risks outweigh the benefits. West's Ann. Cal. Civ. Code § 1714.4 (1983–1984); Idaho Code § 6–1410 (Laws 1986, c. 216). The *Kelley* decision was reversed by Md.Code Art. 27 § 36–I(h) (1992), which provides that a person cannot be held strictly liable for damages resulting from the criminal use of a firearm, unless that person conspires or willfully aids in the commission of the criminal act.

The potential impact of melding strict liability for abnormally dangerous activities with strict products liability is enormous, since many courts do not require that the abnormally dangerous activity involve fault, a defect, or even socially undesirable conduct. Rather, liability for creating an abnormal danger is merely a basis for making a dangerously manufactured product or a dangerous activity pay its way. As the court in *Siegler v. Kuhlman,* supra, said, this liability is a rule of fairness that places the burden of loss "upon the one of the two innocent parties whose acts instigated or made the harm possible." It is similar to the principle of nuisance liability for the intentional violation of another's interest in the use and enjoyment of land, for which liability is imposed (i.e., the invasion is "unreasonable") if "the harm caused by the conduct is serious and the financial burden of compensating for this and similar harm to others would not make the continuation of the conduct [infeasible]." Rest. 2d of Torts § 826(b).

## 3.  MISREPRESENTATION

### a.  Express Warranty

Section 2–313 of the UCC provides:

(1) Express warranties by the seller are created as follows:

(a) Any affirmation of fact or promise made by the seller to the buyer which relates to the goods and becomes part of the basis of the bargain creates an express warranty that the goods shall conform to the affirmation or promise.

(b) Any description of the goods which is made part of the basis of the bargain creates an express warranty that the goods shall conform to the description.

(c) Any sample or model which is made part of the basis of the bargain creates an express warranty that the whole of the goods shall conform to the sample or model.

(2) It is not necessary to the creation of an express warranty that the seller use formal words such as "warrant" or "guarantee" or that he have a specific intention to make a warranty, but an affirmation merely of the value of the goods or a statement purporting to be merely the

seller's opinion or commendation of the goods does not create a warranty.

The section is not limited to statements made by business sellers; anyone can make an express warranty.

Comment 3 to the section says that "no particular reliance" on the statements is required "in order to weave them into the fabric of the agreement. Rather, any fact which is to take such affirmations, once made, out of the agreement requires clear affirmative proof. The issue normally is one of fact." A statement of opinion may become an express warranty where it is reasonable to rely on such a statement. Lovington Cattle Feeders, Inc. v. Abbott Labs. (1982) (statement that defendant's cattle vaccine was as good as the one plaintiff was using).

In Cipollone v. Liggett Group, Inc. (1990) the court held it was sufficient for the plaintiff, in order to prove reliance, to show that she had "read, seen or heard the advertisements at issue." The burden then shifted to the defendant to show that the plaintiff had not read, seen or heard the advertisements, or "did not believe the safety assurance contained therein."

Although there is a division of authority, a number of courts hold that an express warranty may become a basis of the bargain after the sale has been made. Annot., 47 ALR 4th 200 (1986). Comment 7 to § 2–313 contemplates that language used "after the closing of the deal" may become part of the bargain "if it is otherwise reasonable and in order." The court in Green v. A.B. Hagglund and Soner (1986) held conversely that an express warranty may arise before the deal is concluded, with regard to a statement concerning an all-terrain vehicle taken for a "test drive." To reach a contrary conclusion "would allow a seller to escape liability simply because the accident occurs before the purchase is consummated." The court found in the alternative that "[t]echnically speaking, a bargain has been struck when the potential buyer agrees to test drive the vehicle." But see the contrary restrictive holding in Mason v. General Motors Corp. (1986) (no implied warranty on vehicle bailed to plaintiff for test-driving).

An express warranty has been used as a basis for disregarding the privity requirement. Baxter v. Ford Motor Co. (1932). This is true even when the only damage incurred is solely economic loss, as in Randy Knitwear, Inc. v. American Cyanamid Co. (1962).

The liability for breach of an express warranty is a strict liability. No defect need be shown, other than the breach of the warranty itself resulting in proximate injury to the plaintiff.

In an unusual decision, the California Supreme Court held in Brown v. Superior Court (1988) that an action for breach of express warranty would not lie against a manufacturer of a prescription drug that is considered "unavoidably unsafe" (comment *k* to Rest. 2d of Torts). This holding is in conflict with the general recognition that an express warranty gives rise to strict liability by virtue of the representation itself.

## b.  Strict Tort

Section 402B of the Rest. 2d of Torts states:

One engaged in the business of selling chattels who, by advertising, labels, or otherwise, makes to the public a misrepresentation of a material fact concerning the character or quality of a chattel sold by him is subject to liability for physical harm to a consumer of the chattel caused by justifiable reliance upon the misrepresentation, even though

(a) it is not made fraudulently or negligently, and

(b) the consumer has not bought the chattel from or entered into any contractual relation with the seller.

This section parallels the strict liability of express warranty, but it also differs in several respects.  The defendant must be "in the business" of selling chattels, or products, for the section to apply.  This restriction parallels that for the implied warranty of merchantability, and for implied strict tort products liability.  But there is no requirement that one who gives an express warranty be in the business of selling.  A casual or one-time seller can give a valid express warranty.

A § 402B misrepresentation is one that the business seller "makes to the public", while an express warranty—whether by a business or a nonbusiness seller—can be made privately, or between two persons. Presumably a public misrepresentation is something like an advertisement, a sales brochure, or a statement made to the public at large. There is potential for overlap here, however, since a boilerplate express warranty made repeatedly to individual buyers, for example, may have the character of a public representation.

Sec. 402B by its terms applies only to liability for "physical harm to a consumer of the chattel." It is unclear whether recovery would be extended to physical harm to users and bystanders, as with strict tort under § 402A, since there have been few reported cases tried under § 402B. At least one case, Haynes v. American Motors Corp. (1982), read § 402B restrictively to prohibit recovery for physical harm to the consumer's property.

Rest. 2d of Torts § 552C provides for recovery for loss of the difference between the sum parted with and the value received, caused by innocent misrepresentation "in a sale, rental or exchange transaction." This section has no requirement of public misrepresentation, and comment *d* to the section indicates that recovery thereunder is restricted to parties in privity of contract. The Tennessee Supreme Court in Ford Motor Co. v. Lonon (1966) allowed recovery under an earlier draft of this section, 552D, for all economic damages suffered based on public misrepresentation without privity of contract, but this decision was overruled by First Nat. Bank v. Brooks Farms (1991).

Section 402B requires reliance, and in this respect it may differ from the "basis of the bargain" requirement of express warranty. The plaintiff in American Safety Equip. Corp. v. Winkler (1982) was denied recovery under § 402B because the court found he had not relied on defendant's misrepresentation. Reliance can be on pictorial representations, as well as on words. Leichtamer v. American Motors Corp. (1981). Comment *j* to § 402B states that the "reliance need not necessarily be that of the consumer who is injured. It may be that of the ultimate purchaser of the chattel, who because of such reliance passes it on to the consumer who is in fact injured, but is ignorant of the misrepresentation."

The warranty considerations of limitation of remedies, notice of breach, statute of limitations, parol evidence rule, and the like, presumably do not apply to an action in strict tort under § 402B. Undoubtedly the drafters of the Restatement were concerned about this difference where solely economic loss is involved, and that may explain why § 552C is drawn so much more narrowly than its earlier draft, § 552D. (See comment *b* to § 552C, implying as much.) If the public representation requirement were retained for tortious innocent misrepresentation involving solely economic loss, however, the more expansive remedies for strict tort might be justified, since a public representation is usually not bargained for and lacks the element of negotiation that should typify warranties.

## F.  OVERLAPPING BASES
## OF LIABILITY

As a general proposition a plaintiff is entitled to plead and prove as many counts or causes of action as she wishes, and is not required to elect or select the theories on which she will proceed.  In products liability, however, owing to the numerous theories on which one can proceed, their similarities, and the advent of products liability statutes that attempt to consolidate the law in this area, some courts have found that one or more of the theories overlap so that the plaintiff's pleadings are restricted in this regard.

Thus, the court in Zacher v. Budd Co. (1986) (multi-piece wheel) stated that "[a]s between strict liability under § 402A and warranty liability, the warranty predicate, 'fitness for ordinary purposes', appears to set a lower liability threshold that is more beneficial to a plaintiff.  It also appears easier for the jury to understand and apply.  However, several courts have held that for the purposes of jury instructions, strict liability claims subsume the warranty claim and have upheld trial courts' refusal to give parallel instructions."  The court found that "although separate implied warranty instructions are favored and may be required in certain cases, it was not reversible error to refuse these instructions in this case." Similarly, the court in Gates v. Standard Brands, Inc. (1986) (food case) concluded that "the *concepts* represented by the labels 'defective condition unreasonably dangerous' and 'unfitness' are identical. Consequently, we hold that a cause of action for breach of an implied warranty of fitness for human consumption has been superseded by the 'buyer oriented' consumer expectations test when determining whether food is defective." Accord, McQuiston v. K–Mart Corp. (1986) (cookie jar lid).

On the other hand, Lee v. Crookston Coca–Cola Bottling Co. (1971) (coke bottle) held that implied warranty and strict tort are different because the latter requires proof of defect. Accord, Malawy v. Richards Mfg. Co. (1986) (bone plate implantation). In Hartman v. Opelika Machine & Weld. Co. (1982) (industrial machinery), the court held both theories should be charged because of the "unreasonable danger" requirement in strict tort and the differing measures of damages.

It is apparent that the implied warranty of fitness for a particular purpose is different from merchantability and strict tort, since the fitness warranty turns on the existence of special expectations induced by the seller. Merchantability may apply although strict tort may not, where there is only economic damage. Beyond these considerations, the question of whether separate claims in merchantability and implied strict tort should be allowed in the ordinary physical injury products case turns on questions of policy. Allowing separate claims gives the plaintiff a greater chance of recovery, but a proliferation of similar counts may tend to prolong the case and confuse the jury.

The Sixth Circuit in Bogorad v. Eli Lilly & Co. (1985) (DES) held that in a negligent design case there is no need to charge separately on breach of implied warranty, because the theories of strict liability and negligence are essentially the same in design cases. Accord, Prentis v. Yale Mfg. Co. (1984) (forklift). In Randall v. Warnaco, Inc. (1982) (tent fire), on the other hand, the court held that separate charges in negligence and strict liability are required in a design case since negligence focuses on the conduct of the defendant while strict liability focuses on the condition of the product. Resolution of this dispute depends on the view taken of strict liability in design cases, as discussed in Chapter I on the issue of defectiveness.

The courts have not faced the possible overlap between breach of express warranty and innocent tortious misrepresentation. These theories need not overlap, if as pointed out above the "public representation" nature of the tort is emphasized while the "bargained-for" aspect of express warranty is treated as an essential aspect of that theory. Innocent misrepresentation, in both tort and warranty, is clearly distinguishable from negligent and reckless misrepresentation, because in strict liability for product misrepresentation fault is irrelevant. Negligence differs from recklessness in the possible availability of punitive damages for the latter, as well as the possible unavailability of certain defenses such as contributory negligence where recklessness is charged.

There is a possible overlap between express and implied remedies. The implied warranty of merchantability, for example, includes express representations on container packaging and labeling, UCC § 2–314(2)(e)–(f). The express warranty includes warranties of description and sample, which under earlier sales law were treated as implied warranties, § 2–313, comment 1. As noted in Chapter I, courts have held, for example in Greenman v. Yuba Power Products, Inc. (1963), and Santor v. A & M Karagheusian, Inc. (1965), that an implied representation of safety and suitability accompanies a product as a result of its presence on the market.

The tension between implied and express representations runs throughout the law of products liability, and provides a healthy incentive to growth. At the outer extremes the two remain as distinct as colors in the rainbow; but where they come together they tend to meld, just as do the rainbow colors.

Finally, the two great bodies of strict tort law, products liability and abnormally dangerous activities, stand in uneasy tension. Liability for abnormally dangerous activities focuses on conduct or causation rather than on defectiveness. There is no clear definition of what is an abnormally dangerous activity, and the concept can be extended to include products liability based on causation without proof of defect.

## G.  DAMAGES

### 1.  IN GENERAL

A plaintiff is usually entitled to recover all foreseeable damages in a products liability suit based on tort. Some courts may restrict consequential damages recoverable in warranty to those within the contemplation of the parties at the time they entered into the contract, relying on the early landmark English contract case of Hadley v. Baxendale (1854). It is widely held that punitive damages are not recoverable for breach of contract, unless the breach involves the commission of an independent tort. The general rule is that prejudgment interest is not allowable in a personal injury action, but the court in Cavnar v. Quality Control Parking, Inc. (1985) allowed such interest.

Damages, whether in tort or warranty, must be foreseeable. Thus the Florida court in Doyle v. Pillsbury Co. (1985) held that a plaintiff who observed an insect in a can of defendant's food, and fell over in fright, could not recover for resulting injuries because the food had not been ingested and the injuries were therefore unforeseeable. This case should be contrasted with the more egregious fact pattern of Prejean v. Great Atlantic & Pacific Tea Co. (1984), where the plaintiff recovered for stomach tissue tearing and blood loss caused by retching when she unwrapped rotten meat sold by the defendant.

A number of courts allow recovery for emotional distress suffered on witnessing the tortious injury of a close relative, Shepard v. Superior Court (1977), or even a close friend, Kately v. Wilkinson (1983), but apparently all courts require that the shock be suffered at about the same time and place as the other person's injury, Cohen v. McDonnell Douglas Corp. (1983) (nonwitness suffering emotional distress seven hours after the accident cannot recover).

As will be discussed in Chapter IV, there is considerable division of authority regarding the recoverability of solely economic loss in products liability, and the theory on which it should be recovered. Also, as discussed in that chapter, the law varies widely concerning the disclaimability and limitability of damages in products liability.

Some states have enacted statutes placing a cap or limit on the amount of noneconomic damages that can be recovered in a lawsuit. Such damages include recovery for pain and suffering, emotional distress, and punitive or exemplary damages. Some of these statutes have been struck down as unconstitutional, as for example the $875,000 New Hampshire limitation on noneconomic damages that was declared unconstitutional under that state's equal protection constitutional provision, in Brannigan v. Usitalo (1991).


## 2.  EMOTIONAL DISTRESS

There is a division of authority as to whether recovery for emotional distress alone is allowable, where there is no accompanying physical injury. The Massachusetts and Rhode Island courts, in Payton v. Abbott Labs (1982), and Plummer v. Abbott Labs. (1983), held that the plaintiff daughters of mothers who had ingested DES while the plaintiffs were in utero could not recover for fear of contracting cancer in the future, where there was no present physical injury. But a federal district court in Maine held, In re Moorenovich (1986), that workers exposed to asbestos could recover for fear of contracting cancer in the future as the result of such exposure, even though there was no present physical injury. The court also indicated that "[a]ny such damages would be for *present* damages, and we do not believe that a plaintiff's cause of action for cancer, should it ultimately develop, would be necessarily foreclosed by *res judicata* under our ruling." Also, courts have held that recovery for emotional distress without physical injury is permissible where the defendant's conduct is intentional or outrageous. Wisniewski v. Johns–Manville Corp. (1987) (asbestos).

A distinction is drawn between recovery for fear of future injury, and recovery for the risk of the injury itself. Some courts will not allow recovery for the risk (as opposed to fear) of future injury, even where the chance that the risk will result in injury is greater than 50%. Eagle–Picher Indus., Inc. v. Cox (1985) (asbestos). Others allow recovery if the risk is more probable than not, Gideon v. Johns–Manville Sales Corp. (1985) (asbestos), but deny recovery if the risk is not a reasonable medical probability, Devlin v. Johns–Manville Corp. (1985) (damages for fear allowed).

The courts are divided on whether there can be recovery for loss of parental or filial consortium. Compare Powell v. American Motors Corp. (1992) (no such recovery) with Masaki v. General Motors Corp. (1989) (recovery for loss of consortium of an adult child.)

In Volkswagen of America, Inc. v. Dillard (1991) the plaintiff was allowed to recover in warranty for mental anguish associated with the purchase of a new car that was defective and had to be repeatedly repaired. The court said these damages were included within the term "injury to person" under UCC § 2–715(2)(b).

## 3. PUNITIVE DAMAGES

Perhaps no subject in tort law has generated more heated controversy in recent years than the recoverability of punitive damages in tort, including products liability. The evidence indicates that only a small fraction of cases result in punitive

damages, and many of these are business torts
rather than personal injury cases. A few cases
have received disproportionate attention, however,
and the specter of potentially large punitive recoveries has probably contributed significantly to substantial increases in products liability insurance
premiums, as well as to the enactment at the state
level of various restrictions on punitive recoveries.
The statutory restrictions vary widely, from raising
the burden of proof to clear and convincing evidence, to requiring actual malice, to placing a cap
on the amount of recovery, to requiring bifurcation
of trial of the compensatory and punitive aspects of
a case, to requiring managerial involvement in the
misconduct, to requiring part of the recovery to be
paid to the state, and other variations. One must
consult the state statutes in each case to determine
what restrictions, if any, exist.

One of the major concerns has been so-called
mass tort litigation—situations involving such
products as asbestos, Agent Orange, DES, Dalkon
Shield, gas tank positioning, and the like, where a
single product line may generate hundreds or thousands of lawsuits. The multiple litigation for asbestos and Dalkon Shield products resulted in the
Chapter 11 bankruptcy for such industrial giants
as the Johns–Manville Corp. and A. H. Robins Co.
However, there is no indication that these bank-
ruptcies were precipitated by the award of punitive—as opposed to compensatory—damages.

The court in Fischer v. Johns–Manville Corp.
(1986) extensively reviewed the policy reasons for

and against imposing punitive damages in mass tort litigation, and upheld the propriety of awarding such damages. It saw no unfairness to speculative investors, and no indication that such awards would have catastrophic effects on the defendant. It found its decision to be in line with the overwhelming weight of authority. See also the extensive discussion in Jackson v. Johns–Manville Sales Corp. (1986) (9–5 en banc decision upholding the award of punitive damages in asbestos litigation).

The Sixth Circuit, rejecting the "overkill" and finite-resources arguments against imposing punitive damages in the context of multiple litigation, upheld the award of such damages in an asbestos suit, saying: "[W]e do not believe that the Tennessee Supreme Court would proscribe the availability of punitive damages merely because the defendant's alleged tortious behavior resulted in harm to a large number of people." Cathey v. Johns–Manville Sales Corp. (1985). The court in City of Greenville v. W.R. Grace & Co. (1986) allowed $1,591,000 in compensatory damages for the cost of removing city hall asbestos fireproofing, plus $2 million punitive damages representing .0007% of defendant's net worth. An award of $7.5 million in punitive damages was sustained in the Dalkon Shield case of Tetuan v. A.H. Robins Co. (1987).

Punitive damages are awardable based on the wealth and reprehensible conduct of the defendant, Morris v. Parke, Davis & Co. (1983) (DPT). Postmanufacture indifference of the defendant goes to the issue of malice, Maxey v. Freightliner Corp. (1982). Neither compliance with industry custom, *Maxey,* nor compliance with federal safety standards, Wolmer v. Chrysler Corp. (1985), Dorsey v. Honda Motor Co. Ltd. (1981), precludes an award of punitive damages. Oregon has provided by statute, however, that the manufacturer of a drug that is manufactured and labeled in accordance with FDA licensing or regulation standards cannot be held liable for punitive damages unless the manufacturer knowingly withholds material information from the FDA or from the prescribing physician. Or. Rev. Stat. Ch. 774 (1987). Proof of negligence is not enough to sustain recovery for punitive damages. Martin v. Johns–Manville Corp. (1985). The court in O'Gilvie v. International Playtex, Inc. (1987) (toxic shock syndrome) held that the trial court committed reversible error in granting a remittitur of the jury's $10 million punitive damage award, where the remittitur was based on the defendant's post-trial promise and decision to remove its highly absorbent tampon from the market.

Plaintiff may, but is not required to, introduce evidence of the defendant's wealth to aid the fact finder in determining what punitive damages, if any, are appropriate, Vossler v. Richards Mfg. Co., Inc. (1983). Evidence of defendant's insurance is not admissible on the punitive damage issue, however, Michael v. Cole (1979), although such damages are usually insurable.

Punitive damages can be imposed on successor corporations for the recklessness of their predecessors, 55 ALR 4th 166 (1987). The general rule, however, is that public entities such as municipal corporations cannot be held liable for punitive damages. While compensatory damages are not taxable as income, punitive damages do constitute taxable income for federal income tax purposes, Rev. Rul. 84–108, 1984–29 I.R.B.

The United States Supreme Court upheld the award of punitive damages against constitutional due process attack in the non-products liability case of Pacific Mut. Life Ins. Co. v. Haslip (1991). A number of lower courts have upheld against constitutional attack multiple punitive damage awards in products liability mass tort litigation, e.g., Johnson v. Celotex Corp. (1990).

## 4.  JOINT AND SEVERAL LIABILITY

Another area in which extensive efforts have been made to modify the common law by statute is with regard to joint liability—whereby one tortfeasor is held liable for all damages suffered by a claimant, even though other tortfeasors may also have contributed to the injury. If the damages are readily divisible, the tortfeasor would normally be liable only for his share; but liability for the full amount of damages (joint liability) is usually imposed when the damages are practically indivisible, as is often the case when there are multiple tortfeasors. The problem would be minimized if a tortfeasor could obtain contribution from other tortfeasors; but contribution is not available in all jurisdictions, and even when it is available a co-tortfeasor may be immune, insolvent, unidentifiable or not subject to service of process.

A number of states have passed statutes abolishing joint liability generally, or under specified circumstances as for example where the defendant is responsible for less than a certain percent of damages, or they have abolished joint liability for certain types of damages such as for pain and suffering recovery. Instead of joint liability in these situations, the defendant is held liable only severally for her degree of fault—or her degree of causation, in some jurisdictions.

If the plaintiff is innocent, then as between an innocent plaintiff and a culpable defendant it makes sense for the defendant to bear the risk of nonrecovery against a co-tortfeasor. Where both plaintiff and defendant are at fault, and the plaintiff is able to recover under comparative fault as is the rule in most jurisdictions, then arguably there is no more reason to place the risk of nonrecovery on the defendant than the plaintiff. California nevertheless retained joint liability in this situation, in American Motorcycle Ass'n v. Superior Court of Los Angeles County (1978), reasoning that the fault of a plaintiff toward herself is not tortious. California subsequently abolished joint liability by statute for noneconomic damages (pain and suffering and the like).  West's Ann. Cal. Civ. Code § 1431.2 (Fair Responsib. Act of 1986).

Even where both plaintiff and defendant are at fault, the responsibility of another tortfeasor can be divided between the plaintiff and defendant in proportion to their degrees of fault, instead of being placed entirely on one party.  This is the approach of the Uniform Compar. Fault Act, § 2(d), 12 U.L.A. 41.  In addition, it may be appropriate to retain joint liability for the defendant in some situations, as for example where the defendant is wilfully at fault, is engaged in a conspiracy or concert of action, or is vicariously liable.  In these situations, policies based on greater fault and inseparability of claims indicate that joint liability should be imposed on the defendant.  Indeed, the foreseeability of cotortfeasor misconduct argues in favor of retaining joint liability generally.

# CHAPTER III

## THE PARTIES
### A. PLAINTIFFS

Except for a few jurisdictions that still require privity of contract for an action in warranty, a plaintiff may sue any products defendant on any available theory to recover for personal injuries. Plaintiff need not be a buyer, user or consumer, and any foreseeable plaintiff including bystanders can recover. As the court in Elmore v. American Motors Corp. (1969) said: "If anything, bystanders should be entitled to greater protection than the consumer or user where injury to bystanders is reasonably foreseeable. Consumers and users, at least, have the opportunity to inspect for defects and to limit their purchases to articles manufactured by reputable manufacturers and sold by reputable retailers, whereas the bystander ordinarily has no such opportunities."

An area in which bystander litigation may develop significantly in the future concerns nonsmokers who are subjected to cigarette smoke from smokers. A suit against cigarette manufacturers in such a situation cannot be effectively met with the usual defense of assumption of the risk, which is available against smokers. There have been

83

cases permitting an employee to sue her employer to obtain an injunction against exposing the employee to cigarette smoke in the workplace. Annot., 37 ALR 4th 480 (1985).

Several states and state subdivisions have passed statutes, ordinances or regulations prohibiting or restricting smoking in public places. E.g., Ariz. Rev. Stat. § 36–601.01; 11 Minn. Stat. Ann. § 144.-411–144.417; Vernon's Tex. Code Ann., Penal Code § 48.01(a). Violation of such statutes might be used as evidence not only in an action against smokers, but also against cigarette manufacturers who can reasonably foresee such violations. The existence of such statutes also indicates the growing public reaction against smoking, and this reaction will likely tend toward manufacturer liability for injuries and deaths attributable to smoking.

Persons who suffer from witnessing the tortious injury of a close relative, Shepard v. Superior Court (1977) (auto accident), or a close friend, Kately v. Wilkinson (1983) (water-skiing accident), can recover for resulting injuries. While some courts have required that plaintiff's emotional distress be accompanied by physical injury, others have held that emotional distress alone is sufficient, Culbert v. Sampson's Supermarkets Inc. (1982) (plaintiff's child choked on defendant's baby food). Probably all courts, however, require the mental or physical injury to occur at about the same time and place as the injury to the relative or friend, Cohen v. McDonnell Douglas Corp. (1983) (airplane crash—

nonwitness who learned of accident 7 hours later could not recover).

Rescuers of persons injured by defective products are widely permitted to recover against the product manufacturer or seller for injuries incurred in the attempted rescue, Guarino v. Mine Safety Appl. Co. (1969) (oxygen-type protective mask). One court held that the rescue must be spontaneous, and that a deliberate rescuer could not recover. Bobka v. Cook County Hosp. (1981) (skin graft donor unforeseeable). This holding makes little sense, since a deliberate rescue probably requires more bravery and is more commendable than a spontaneous one. Cf. Cords v. Anderson (1977) (non-products case—rescuer's injury, on descent into gorge 15 minutes after friend's fall, held actionable). The majority rule holds that an injury suffered in a reasonable attempt to rescue property is actionable. Caldwell v. Ford Motor Co. (1981) (defective truck on fire—plaintiff injured in removing property from truck bed).

The majority rule is that a professional rescuer cannot recover in products liability for a foreseeable risk caused by the product unless the defendant is guilty of wilful, wanton misconduct, Mahoney v. Carus Chem. Co., Inc. (1986), or unless the hazard is unusual or hidden, Hawkins v. Sunmark Industries, Inc. (1986). Some courts, however, hold that the rule denying recovery to a professional rescuer (the Fireman's Rule) is intended to protect only land occupiers, and does not bar recovery against a product manufacturer, e.g., Court v. Grzelinski (1978).

For recovery for fear of future injury, and the risk of future injury, see the section on damages in the preceding chapter. Recovery for solely economic loss is dealt with in the next chapter.

Opening up products liability for personal injuries to include all foreseeable plaintiffs—not just buyers, or buyers in privity of contract with the seller—has an expansive effect on products liability law in general. It also has the policy impact of applying pressure at the other end of the relation, to expand the category of defendants in products liability so as to include others than just products sellers. As can be seen in the remainder of this chapter, the tendency to expand the category of defendants is a notable characteristic of the developing law of products liability.

## B. DEFENDANT SELLERS OF NEW PRODUCTS

### 1. MANUFACTURERS

Manufacturers can be sued on any of the theories discussed in the previous chapter. Not only can the final assembler be sued, but a manufacturer of a component part can be sued as well if the part is defective when it leaves the component manufacturer's hands, or if the specifications for the component obviously indicate that it will be dangerous when incorporated into the finished product, Estate of Carey v. Hy–Temp Mfg., Inc. (1991). Here, questions of foreseeability often arise. For example, in Thomas v. Kaiser Agric. Chem. (1980), the manufacturer of an adaptor was aware that its product would be used on liquid-fertilizer applicators where it posed an especial danger, and could therefore be held liable for defective design even though the component could be used safely for other purposes. If the component supplier is unaware of and has no control over subsequent uses, it will probably not be liable, Walker v. Stauffer Chem. Corp. (1971) (sulfuric acid subsequently dangerously mixed with alkaline base). In some cases, as in Verge v. Ford Motor Co. (1978), the component manufacturer will not be liable since the component has multiple uses and a safety device (here, a backup signal on a truck cab and chassis) could not be properly installed until the time of final assembly. The component supplier may be liable even if the component is changed during the process of assembly, as long as the change does not substantially alter the component. Union Supply Co. v. Pust (1978) (defendant provider of conveyor mechanical design, which was combined with the performance design of another).

Section 400 of the Rest. 2d of Torts states: "One who puts out as his own product a chattel manufactured by another is subject to the same liability as though he were the manufacturer." Thus, under this section a manufacturer can be held liable for the negligence of a component supplier, Ford Motor Co. v. Mathis (1963), and a retailer for the negligence of a manufacturer, Slavin v. Francis H. Leggett & Co. (1935). This section will apply unless the real manufacturer is "clearly and accurately identified on the label or other markings on the goods." Rest. 2d of Torts § 400, comment *d*. The rule may be important where the retailer cannot be sued unless it is treated as a manufacturer, or where the plaintiff wishes to show the negligence of one supplier and attribute it to another.

Section 400 has been used as a basis for imposing strict liability against a retailer, who would not otherwise be thus held liable, Pierce v. Liberty Furniture Co., Inc. (1977), and for imposing strict liability against a licensor that permits products to be identified by the licensor's trademark, Carter v. Joseph Bancroft & Sons Co. (1973).

In Morris v. American Motors Corp. (1982), § 400 was applied to hold a manufacturer liable for another's negligent manufacture of a component part (solenoid in starter) that was installed by an authorized dealer during the period of the manufacturer's express warranty. "AMC held itself out as responsible for this car until the warranty period was up." It was reasonable for the plaintiff "to have believed the replacement solenoid was an integral part of his American Motors Corporation-backed car when he drove it away from the dealership after servicing."

A manufacturer can be liable for the downstream misassembly of a product by a dealer, Caporale v. Raleigh Indus. of America, Inc. (1980) (bicycle), Sabloff v. Yamaha Motor Co. (1971) (motorcycle), even though the unassembled product was not defective when it left the manufacturer's hands. Presumably this rule would apply to the misassembly of an unassembled product by a consumer as well, and it could also perhaps include nonmanufacturing sellers as defendants. The rule might run into problems in jurisdictions where by statute, e.g. Tenn. Code Ann. § 29–28–105(a), or by court decision in order to impose liability the product is required to be defective when it leaves the manufacturer's or seller's hands. The date-of-defect issue could be met in this context, however, by imputing the later-occurring defect to the manufacturer or seller by a relation-back approach similar to that used in property law.

## 2.  MIDDLEMEN AND RETAILERS

The various theories of recovery discussed in Chapter II, including strict liability, apply to all sellers in the chain of distribution. It may not be possible to prove negligence against a nonmanufacturing seller, since the majority view is that such sellers are mere conduits with no affirmative duty to inspect or test for latent defects. However, if the retailer does undertake to inspect, test, or assemble a product, it may be liable for failing to do so with reasonable care. Bower v. Corbell (1965) (negligently tested power saw). In Lakeman

v. Otis Elev. Co. (1991) the court held that the bulk supplier of a cleaning solvent assumed the duty of warning ultimate users by voluntarily reviewing the warning labels of its distributors.

There are some cases holding that a retailer, and presumably any middleman, cannot be held liable in implied strict liability (breach of the warranty of merchantability, or strict tort under Rest. 2d of Torts § 402A) for selling a defective product in a sealed container. Sam Shainberg Co. v. Barlow (1972). The sealed container doctrine is a term of art used to relieve nonmanufacturing sellers of implied strict liability for latent defects not discoverable by reasonable inspection, Parker v. Ford Motor Co. (1976), whether or not the product is sold in a sealed container. A few jurisdictions have adopted the doctrine by statute. It does not apply, however, to bar recovery for breach of the warranty of fitness for a particular purpose, Maze v. Bush Bros. (1971), for violation of pure food statutes, White v. E. Tenn. Pack. Co. (1947), or presumably for misrepresentation, since in these situations the seller or the statute creates special expectations and rights. Some jurisdictions by statute release the nonmanufacturing seller from strict liability where the manufacturer is solvent and can be sued. See, e.g., Tenn. Code Ann. § 29–28–106 (release from strict tort liability). But if a party undertakes to repair or rebuild a product, he may be treated as if he were its manufacturer. Anderson v. Olmsted Util. Equip., Inc. (1991).

The court in Coyle v. Richardson–Merrell, Inc. (1991) refused to extend strict products liability to a pharmacist supplying a prescription drug. It said the risks and benefits of such a product "are to be assessed only by licensed physicians acting on behalf of particular patients whose individual physical condition and circumstances are known to them." It noted that the clear weight of authority was in accord with this holding.

A wholesaler, Southern of Rocky Mount, Inc. v. Woodward Spec. Sales, Inc. (1981), or a sales agent, Hoffman v. Loos & Dilworth, Inc. (1982), can be held strictly liable for the sale of defective goods even though the goods pass directly from the manufacturer to the ultimate buyer with the intermediary only receiving a commission on the sale. Most cases hold, however, that a mere financing lessor of a product, Nath v. National Equip. Leasing Corp. (1981), should not be held strictly liable. California held a lending bank, with the right of construction supervision, liable for failure to prevent negligent construction by a real estate developer, in Connor v. Great Western Sav. & Loan Ass'n (1968). The decision was promptly overruled by statute, West's Ann. Cal. Civ. Code § 3434.

In Weber v. Johns–Manville Corp. (1986), the court denied defendant Pacor's motion for summary judgment in an asbestos suit based on strict liability for failure to warn. The records indicated "that between 1960 and 1972 Pacor participated as an intermediary of some sort in Carbide's purchase of approximately 3.5 million pounds of raw asbestos products from Canadian Johns–Manville." Affidavits filed by Pacor stated that it "never delivered any asbestos fiber or products to Union Carbide" and that "Pacor's only involvement in the transaction was to receive orders which were forwarded to the miner, to send invoices and to insure the forwarding of the proper funds." The court further found that there was "nothing to indicate that the asbestos in question passed through Pacor's hands at any time".

Nevertheless, the court found that the defendant was "not an *ordinary* broker" and was "more than a blind order-taker." It was "intimately involved in the asbestos industry for a number of years as a contractor, distributor, and fabricator". Its familiarity with the hazards of the industry was "evidenced by its practice of requiring employees working in areas of excessive dust concentration to wear protective devices and respirators". Additionally, New Jersey "has clearly rejected the requirement that a technical sale occur before strict liability will be imposed". Therefore, the court found a "sufficient causative relationship" between the defendant and the product to justify overruling the summary judgment motion, since "Pacor—whether considered a seller, distributor, or a provider of services—arranged and profited from the supply of millions of pounds of raw asbestos packaged in its original and unchanged condition".

A broker who received no commission on the sale of a product was held not strictly liable in Dillard

Dept. Stores v. Associated Merchandising Corp. (1989). The court in Oscar Mayer Corp. v. Mincing Trading Corp. (1990) held that a broker was not a product seller.

## C.  DEFENDANT USED–PRODUCTS SELLERS

Some courts hold that a seller cannot be held strictly liable for the sale of used goods (if there is no misrepresentation), where the defect arises while the product is in the possession of a previous unknown owner and is not due to any flaw in manufacture or design.  Grimes v. Axtell Ford Lincoln–Mercury (1987) (defective used axle purchased by defendant dealer from salvage yard).  If the seller of a used car were held strictly liable in this situation, the Illinois Supreme Court said in Peterson v. Lou Bachrodt Chev. Co. (1975) (bad brakes), the "dealer would in effect become an insurer against defects which had come into existence after the chain of distribution was completed, and while the product was in the control of one or more consumers."  The reasoning of these cases seems to turn on the idea that the retailer should not be strictly liable unless it has an action over against its supplier, since where it has such an action over it can force its supplier to "correct or prevent the manufacture of dangerously defective products."  Nelson v. Nelson Hdwr., Inc. (1991).

The court in Musser v. Vilsmeier Auction Co. (1989) held that an auctioneer could not be found strictly liable for the auction sale of a defective product, since the auctioneer was "not equipped to pass on the quality of the goods" and had no "direct impact on" or "continuing relationship" with the manufacturer. The dissent argued that the majority was "erroneously injecting concepts of negligence" into strict liability, and that the extension of strict liability to the auctioneer would serve as an incentive to safety.

While some courts refuse to impose strict liability on the commercial seller of used products, on the ground that such a seller "does not offer, and the buyer does not expect, either implied or express representations of quality," Peterson v. Idaho First Nat. Bank (1990), the clear majority impose strict liability on such a seller. The "nonoccasional or regular seller of a used product ... like sellers of new products, [has] assumed a special responsibility to the public, may spread the loss caused by defective products and [has] the ability and knowledge to remove defects before placing the used product in the distribution chain." Stiles v. Batavia Atomic Horseshoes, Inc. (1992).

## D. DEFENDANT SUCCESSOR COR-PORATIONS OF PRODUCTS SELLERS

There are a number of cases testing whether one entity, B, that purchases the business of another, A, can be held strictly liable vicariously for injuries caused after the business purchase by a defective product sold by A before the purchase. The issue normally arises in the context of a *corporate* business purchase, although the principles can be applied to other business entities such as associations, partnerships and sole proprietorships. The successor, B—if not liable vicariously—will normally not be liable otherwise unless a duty to warn arises as discussed in Chapter VI owing to the successor's undertaking to service customer accounts of the predecessor thus becoming aware of dangerous products used by the customer that were purchased from the predecessor.

The doctrine of successor corporate liability, as it has come to be called, has its roots in corporate law as a device to protect dissenting stockholders in corporate sellouts. It has been adapted to products law, however, as a device to protect injured consumers, and as such the courts have not felt constrained by corporate rules in determining liability.

The corporate rule was that when A sold its entire business to B in exchange for stock of B, and then A dissolved leaving B carrying on the business of A, this transaction would be treated as a de facto merger with B assuming by law the obligations of A. See Nissen Corp. v. Miller (1991). The requirement that the exchange be for stock is often replaced by a rule that an exchange for stock, cash or other property is sufficient. Turner v. Bituminous Cas. Co. (1976). Sometimes the rule of successor liability is applied because the consideration for the exchange is inadequate. See Ray v. Alad Corp. (1977). Courts often require that there be a continuity of management personnel or of ownership from A to B, in order for successor liability to be imposed. Florom v. Elliott Mfg. (1989) (management personnel); Cilurso v. Premier Crown Corp. (1991) (ownership).

Two principal *products liability* rules have developed for imposing corporate successor liability, one called the continuity-of-enterprise or mere-continuation rule of *Turner v. Bituminous Cas. Co.,* and the other the product-line rule of *Ray v. Alad Corp.* The *Turner* rule requires: 1) continuity of management, personnel, physical location, assets and general business of the predecessor; 2) dissolution of the predecessor as soon as legally and practically possible; 3) assumption by the successor of all liabilities of the predecessor necessary for continuation of normal business operations; and 4) a holding out of itself to the public by the successor as the effective continuation of the predecessor.

The product-line theory of *Ray* applies when the successor acquires all or substantially all the manufacturing assets, and undertakes essentially the same manufacturing operation, of the predecessor. It is based on policies stemming from virtual destruction of remedies against the predecessor through the acquisition, the ability of the successor to spread the risk, and the fairness of requiring it to do so as a burden reasonably attached to the benefit of acquiring the good will of the predecessor.

The Third Circuit refused to impose liability on a successor corporation because such liability ignores the "causal relationship between the defendant's act and the plaintiff's injury—a concept that is fundamental to tort law." Polius v. Clark Equip. Co. (1986). The court felt that the rationale of strict liability "does not logically support expansion of liability merely because the primary tortfeasor is no longer available to pay the judgment."

A division of authority exists as to whether successor liability should be imposed even though the predecessor still exists. The court in LaFountain v. Webb Industries Corp. (1991) refused to impose successor liability primarily because the predecessor continued to exist as a viable business concern against which a potential remedy existed. Other courts have found such continuation of the predecessor no impediment to the imposition of successor liability. Tift v. Forage King Indus., Inc. (1982) (predecessor, a sole proprietorship, still in existence); Nieves v. Bruno Sherman Corp. (1981) (successor and predecessor corporations held jointly liable). The court held, In re White Motor Credit Corp. (1987), that federal bankruptcy law prohibited imposing successor corporation liability on the purchaser of a bankruptcy estate, since such liability would force debtors to accept less on sales thus subverting statutory priorities. Moreover, said the court in Conway v. White Trucks (1989), there exists a special fund in bankruptcy against which the claimant can assert a claim.

It is uncertain to what extent continuance of the product line—or the continuity of management and control, where that is required—must be sustained in substantially the same form by the successor in order for liability to be imposed for products sold by the predecessor. George v. Parke–Davis (1987) held that a successor that carried on the general pharmaceutical business of the predecessor, but did not manufacture the particular product, DES, that caused plaintiff's injury, could not be held liable. On the other hand, in Rawlings v. D.M. Oliver, Inc. (1979), a successor which acquired the general line of business (industrial kelp dryers) of the predecessor, but did not continue the precise line (a customized product) that caused plaintiff's injury, could nevertheless be held liable.

Some courts have held that the successor need not acquire all the predecessor's assets in order to be liable. Liability may be imposed where the successor acquires only one division of the predecessor, if a defective product from that division sold by the predecessor causes injury. Amader v. Pittsburgh Corning Corp. (1982); Gibson v. Armstrong World Indus., Inc. (1986). Contra, Shorb v. Airco, Inc. (1986).

## E. DEFENDANT LESSORS, BAILORS, AND LICENSORS OF PRODUCTS

The landmark case imposing strict liability on the lessor of a product is Cintrone v. Hertz Truck Leasing & Rental Serv. (1965), where the long-term lessor of trucks was held strictly liable for an injurious defect that arose during the term of the lease. As the court said, there is "no good reason" for restricting warranties to sales. It noted that comment 2 of the express warranty section of the UCC, § 2–313, states that "warranties need not be confined either to sales contracts or to the direct parties to such a contract. They may arise in other appropriate circumstances such as in the case of bailments for hire." By means of a bailment, said the court, "parties can often reach the same business ends that can be achieved by selling and buying." The offering of vehicles for hire to the public "necessarily carries with it a representation that they are fit for operation", whether the vehicles are new or used, since "the rental rates are the same whether a new or used vehicle is supplied." As the court in Price v. Shell Oil Co. (1970) put it: "Both lessors and sellers are an 'integral part' of the overall 'marketing enterprise that should bear the cost of injuries resulting from defective products'."

The court in Kemp v. Miller (1990) noted that since *Cintrone* "numerous courts" have adopted the reasoning of that case. In view of the "rapid growth of the commercial leasing industry in recent years", the *Kemp* court followed *Cintrone* in applying strict liability "to those who are engaged in the business of leasing products to the consuming public."

*Cintrone* held strict liability applied to any defective condition in the product arising during the rental period. But a later case from the same jurisdiction, A–Leet Leasing Corp. v. Kingshead Corp. (1977), held that in order for strict liability to be imposed the defect must exist at the beginning of the lease term.

The courts are divided as to whether strict liability should be imposed on the commercial lessor under a short term lease. Recognizing this division of authority, the court in Wilson v. Dover Skating Center, Ltd. (1989) nevertheless imposed strict liability on the owner of a skating rink that leased defective roller skates for use at the rink. It found that the defendant was "in the best position to inspect the skates" and thereby reduce the risk, and to "spread the cost of the risk." The rental of the skates was not an isolated or occasional transaction, but an "essential part of and well within the normal course of defendant's business."

Perhaps the reluctance of some courts to impose strict liability in the short-term lease situation is because they sense the overlap between strict products liability on the one hand, and premises liability on the other hand where negligence is generally the standard of liability. See Shaw v. Fairyland at Harvey's Inc. (1966) (no strict liability against a provider of ferris wheel rides). But strict products liability may eventually be extended generally to the owner of defective business premises open to the public.

One court refused to impose strict liability on the lessor of 20 food-catering-service trucks, because the defendant was not a "mass lessor similar to a manufacturer or retailer." Smith v. Nick's Catering Serv. (1977). Most courts, however, apply strict liability to one in the regular business of selling or leasing products, without regard to the volume of business involved.

The cases differ on whether the commercial lessor of railroad boxcars can be held strictly liable for defects in the leased cars. The court in Torres v. Southern Pac. Transp. Co. (1978) held that strict liability should not be imposed because "the highly specialized industry-use interchange program to be found in this case is too dissimilar to the commercial distribution of a product to warrant the doctrine's application." In Vanskike v. ACF Indus., Inc. (1981), on the other hand, the court imposed strict liability in such a situation, finding the key to be "whether the interchange of railroad cars is a commercial transaction. This is a matter of function rather than mere ownership."

Courts generally do not impose strict liability on a financing lessor who merely "offered the use of money" to enable the lessee to lease a product. The lessor in this situation "neither marketed the [product] nor placed it in the stream of commerce."

Starobin v. Niagara Machine & Tool Works Corp. (1991).

The court in Pacific Nat. Ins. v. Gormsen Appliance (1991) refused to apply strict liability to the commercial lessor of used goods, saying that the "consumer of used property, whether a purchaser or a lesser, seeks economy and practical utility." This holding is contrary to the general rule.

## F. DEFENDANT EMPLOYER– SUPPLIERS OF PRODUCTS

A number of states, by statute or common law, permit a tort action by an employee against her employer—outside the exclusivity provisions of workers' compensation—where the employer engages in intentional misconduct causing injury to the employee. In Gross v. Kenton Structural and Ornamental Ironworks, Inc. (1984) (staircase collapse), for example, the court held that an employee tort action would lie against an employer for failure to warn of a known danger. See also Johns–Manville Prod. Corp. v. Contra Costa Super. Court (1980) (concealment of asbestos-disease diagnosis). The courts differ as to the intent necessary to establish liability.

California by statute permits an employee tort action against an employer that removes or fails to install a point-of-operation guard on a power press, where the absence of the guard creates a probability of serious injury or death. West's Ann.Cal.Labor Code § 4558. A large percentage of products liability actions arise from workplace injuries on industrial machinery, particularly punch or power presses, that lack adequate guards. In such cases, as discussed in the last section of this chapter, the employee will often sue the manufacturer of the workplace machine, who in turn will seek contribution from the employer. California's statute attempts to meet in part the problem of unguarded hazardous power presses by providing a direct action by the employee against the employer.

A workplace tort remedy that has enjoyed very limited success is where the employer supplies the employee with a defective product that the employer also sells to the public at large. See Chaddock v. Johns–Manville Sales Corp. (1984). In this situation the employer has been viewed as acting in the "dual capacity" of a product supplier to his employee, and as such he can be held tortiously liable to the employee. Most courts have rejected this theory of recovery, see Kaess v. Armstrong Cork Co. (1987), and some have done so by statute, e.g., West's Ann.Cal.Labor Code § 3602(a).

It is apparent that the dual capacity doctrine undermines the exclusive-remedy provisions of workers' compensation law. On the other hand, it makes good sense that an employer should be held tortiously liable to an employee when the employer is acting in a non-employer capacity. The difficul-

ty is in separating the overlap between employer
and nonemployer capacities.

## G.  DEFENDANT PROVIDERS
## OF SERVICES
### 1.  IN GENERAL

A number of cases emphasize the service aspect
of a product transaction in reaching the conclusion
that principles of strict liability should not be
applied.  Such a distinction seems artificial, since
all product transactions involve a significant service component.  A product defective in manufacture or design often is defective, for example, because of some service performed or not performed
by the manufacturer.

Sometimes courts take a "predominance" approach:  is the transaction predominantly one of
services, or predominantly one involving the sale of
goods?  Such a test provides no bright line for
analysis, or policy basis for its application.

To the extent that courts are trying to separate a
mixed, or hybrid, transaction into its separate com-
ponents of product and service, the sale-service
distinction has some facial attraction.  Services
can only be performed with or without care, the
reasoning goes, but products can be defective although all due care is exercised in their preparation.  This distinction breaks down, however, except in the situations where defects occur natural-
ly; all other defects are man-made and are the

product of services.   Moreover, the strict liability tests of ordinary consumer expectations and risk-benefit balancing can be applied to judge the adequacy of services as well as of goods.

A number of cases attempt to categorize professional services differently from ordinary services, by refusing to impose strict liability for the rendition of professional services.   Again, the distinction is hard to justify, either conceptually or pragmatically.   Presumably most engineers who work on products at the design and production stage are professionals, although strict liability is imposed for defective design or production.   Moreover, it is difficult to draw defensible distinctions between a professional cosmetician and a professional health care provider, for purposes of deciding whether or not to impose strict liability.

Many of the so-called service-transaction cases involve a significant representational element. Where liability is based on misrepresentation, the cases in the previous chapter indicate that strict liability is regularly imposed.   If, however, the representational aspect of the case is viewed as a failure to warn, or as a failure to investigate or test adequately prior to making the representation, then a court may apply a negligence analysis rather than one of strict liability.

If strict products liability is viewed as encompassing service transactions as well as the sale of goods, there is little reason to treat products liability as distinct from tort law generally.   It could be argued that strict liability should be extended to include all *business* providers of products, objects, and services, on the grounds that a business person is in the best position to prevent injury and to spread the risk of loss. The rationales for representational and abnormal-danger strict liability extend beyond business persons, however, to include anyone engaged in the activity of representing a product, or of conducting an abnormally dangerous activity.

## 2. REPRESENTATIONAL CONDUCT

Product certifiers, Hanberry v. Hearst Corp. (1969), and testers, Hempstead v. General Fire Extinguisher Corp. (1967), have been held liable for negligent certification and testing of another's product. The *Hanberry* court indicated that strict liability would be inappropriate where the defendant only represented "the general design and materials used to be satisfactory", since the general endorser "makes no representation it has examined or tested each item marketed." There seems to be no reason however why the endorser could not be strictly liable for misrepresenting either general design or individual product safety, depending on the nature and scope of the representation. The certifier may certify hundreds and thousands of different products, and in this respect its potential exposure can be significantly greater than that of a manufacturer who only markets a single line of products. This greater potential exposure, however, should not determine whether strict liability ought to be imposed.

In King v. National Spa and Pool Instit. (1990) the court held that if a manufacturer or installer of a pool relied on standards promulgated by a trade association in constructing or installing the pool, the association could be liable if it breached a duty of care in promulgating the standards. It seems that strict liability of the trade association would also be appropriate here, insofar as the safety guides constituted misrepresentations. In Hall v. E.I. Du Pont De Nemours & Co. (1972), the court held negligence and strict liability could be imposed on the trade association of the explosives industry for its role in failing to warn and take other safety measures to prevent blasting cap injuries.

Trademark licensors, Torres v. Goodyear Tire & Rubber Co. (1990), and franchisors, Kosters v. Seven–Up Co. (1979), can be held strictly liable for defective products marketed by licensees and franchisees that follow the trademark and franchise specifications of the defendant. If, however, the licensor is only minimally involved in the manufacture, distribution or sale of the licensee's product, strict liability may not be imposed against the licensor. Burkert v. Petrol Plus of Naugatuck, Inc. (1990).

It is apparent that advertisers can be held liable in negligence or strict liability for misrepresentations made by them concerning the products of another. In Cooga Mooga Inc. et al. (1978), the respondent Pat Boone was required by the FTC to make restitution for false statements in the television endorsement of a cosmetic product. Advertisers will of course take the position that advertising is mere "puffing" and is generally understood to be so; but the tendency is to treat would-be puffing and statements of opinion as actionable, especially when made by one asserting superior knowledge.

## 3. PROFESSIONAL SERVICES

A leading case in which the court refused to impose strict liability on the grounds that the defendant was a provider of professional services is Magrine v. Spector (1969), where the defendant dentist's hypodermic needle broke off in plaintiff's jaw allegedly through no fault of the defendant. In a later case, Newmark v. Gimbel's, Inc. (1969), the court imposed strict liability on a beauty parlor for injuries resulting from the application of a permanent wave solution. It attempted to distinguish *Magrine* by saying: the beautician "is engaged in a commercial enterprise" while the dentist is engaged "in a profession"; the former caters to "a form of aesthetic convenience or luxury" involving "nonprofessional services", while the latter "exercises his best judgment" in rendering services that stem "from a felt necessity of the patient"; the dentist "cannot advertise for patients" (no longer true, in view of First Amendment rulings of the United States Supreme Court).

The basic thrust of the distinction made in *Newmark* appears to be that medical services are more useful than cosmetic services, but this kind of distinction may be hard to justify generally in canvassing the various services available throughout society. It can be argued that medical patients are less suitable ultimate cost bearers than users of non-medical services, but this argument is not determinative in view of the widespread availability of medical insurance.

The court in La Rossa v. Scientific Design Co. (1968) refused to impose strict liability on an engineering company that designed and engineered a plant, including a reactor containing pellets coated with vanadium—a carcinogen—that allegedly killed plaintiff's deceased who was a worker at the plant. The court said that "[p]rofessional services" do not involve the "mass production of goods or a large body of distant consumers whom it would be unfair to require to trace the article they used along the channels of trade to the original manufacturer and there to pinpoint an act of negligence remote from their knowledge and even from their ability to inquire." The plaintiff in this case was unable to "pinpoint an act of negligence", however, since the jury found the defendant free of fault. Insofar as the decision turns on a mass-production rationale, it meets the same problems of definition confronted by some courts in the lease-bailment cases previously considered.

The cases divide over whether a hospital can be held strictly liable for product-related services. In Karibjanian v. Thomas Jefferson Univ. Hosp. (1989) the court held that a hospital could be held strictly liable for death resulting from the injection of thorium dioxide as a contrast medium during a cerebral arteriography, since the hospital regularly supplied the medium to its patients as part of its service operations. But in Hoff v. Zimmer, Inc. (1990) the court held the hospital was not a supplier—within the meaning of strict tort liability—of a surgically implanted hip prosthesis that broke.

The supplying of blood has often been treated as a service rather than a sale, since the "main object" is "health care and treatment." Fisher v. Sibley Mem. Hosp. (1979). Most states by statute relieve suppliers of blood, blood products and human tissue from strict liability. Here the legislatures have made a policy decision to protect blood suppliers from strict liability on the basis of an "unavoidably unsafe" rationale.

A general negligence standard, rather than a professional customary standard of care, was applied to a blood bank in United Blood Services v. Quintana (1992). Contra, Osborn v. Irwin Mem. Blood Bank (1992) (professional standard controls).

### 4.   PURE SERVICE TRANSACTIONS

Where the defendant provides no product, but only services, the court in Nickel v. Hyster Co. (1978) (fork lift truck repair) said the "prevailing view nationwide is that the doctrine of strict products liability is not applicable to providers of services, including repairers." Accord, DeLoach v. Whitney (1981) (no strict liability for the installation of a tire on an existing defective stem not furnished by the defendant). The court in Barry v. Stevens Equip. Co. (1985) (alligator shear machine repair), went even further to hold that a repairer has no duty of care to warn of or correct dangers outside the scope of the work contracted for.

The cases are not uniform, however, in holding the nonselling repairer free from strict liability. In Worrell v. Barnes (1971), it was held that a remodeler could be found strictly liable for the defective installation of gas appliances furnished by another. Similarly, in Gentile By and Through Gentile v. MacGregor Mfg. Co. (1985), the court found that a football helmet repairer could be held strictly liable for a defect not caused by the defendant in a helmet sold by another. These cases seem correct if a product supplier can be held strictly liable for the service—rather than the product—component of its supply, since the presence or absence of a product makes no difference on the issue of the source of liability.

## H.  DEFENDANT REAL ESTATE SUPPLIERS

### 1.  BUILDER–VENDORS

The leading case applying strict liability against the mass builder-vendor of a new home that caused personal injury because of defective construction is Schipper v. Levitt & Sons (1965) (hot water heater without mixing valve).  The court could see "no reason for differentiating mass sales of homes from advertised models, as in the Levitt operation, from mass sales of automobiles...."  The buyer "clearly relies on the skill of the developer and on its implied representation that the house will be erected in [a] reasonably workmanlike manner and will be reasonably fit for habitation."  In McDonald v. Mianecki (1979) (non-potable water), the court extended the *Schipper* reasoning to a business builder-vendor not engaged in mass construction. "Whether the builder be large or small, the purchaser relies upon his superior knowledge and skill, and he impliedly represents that he is qualified to erect a habitable dwelling."

Other courts refuse to impose an implied warranty of habitability against the builder-vendor of new homes, believing that the issue involves a "multitude of competing economic, cultural and societal values" which the legislature rather than the court is more suited to address.  Bruce Farms, Inc. v. Coupe (1978) (cracks in brick veneer).  Presumably such a court would apply either a negligence standard, or the even more restrictive rule requiring proof of fraud or misrepresentation, see Elderkin v. Gaster (1972).

Some courts require privity as a condition to suing in strict liability, or in negligence, for pure economic loss resulting from the purchase of defective premises. See Lempke v. Dagenais (1988), and cases discussed therein. These cases reflect the conflict over recovery for solely economic loss without privity in products liability. See Blagg v. Fred Hunt Co., Inc. (1981). Some real estate cases carry the privity requirement over even to warranty cases involving personal injury, Wright v. Creative Corp. (1972) (injuries from untempered glass— proof of negligence required in the absence of privity), and physical damage to property, Patterson v. Jim Walter Homes (1985) (electrical wiring fire— privity required for implied warranty action).

There are cases refusing to impose strict liability, even for personal injuries, against persons who construct real estate improvements because there is allegedly no product or sale. In Brooks v. Eugene Burger Management Corp. (1989) plaintiff contended defendant's apartment complex was defective because it was not fenced in. The plaintiff was injured when he left the complex and was hit by a car. In denying recovery, the court said the apartment complex was not a product, the absence of a fence was not a defect, and the danger was "obvious and patent." See also Thibos v. Pacific Gas & Elec. Co. (1986) (street lighting a "service", not a product); Held v. 7–Eleven Food Store (1981) (gravel-filled hole in front of store not distributed to public at large).

Thus far the courts have not imposed implied strict liability against professional vendors of realty, i.e., real estate agents. Perhaps this is because the issue has not been raised. The professional nonbuilding vendor is comparable to the nonmanufacturing seller in products liability. There is a division of authority as to whether a real estate broker can be held strictly liable for innocent misrepresentation. Hoffman v. Connall (1987).

## 2. LESSORS

The landmark case of Javins v. First Nat. Realty Corp. (1970) imposed liability on the lessor of urban realty for housing code violations that breached the implied warranty of habitability. "Since the lessees continue to pay the same rent, they were entitled to expect that the landlord would continue to keep the premises in their beginning condition during the lease term." In Fair v. Negley (1978), the court found an implied warranty of habitability without regard to whether there were housing code violations, noting "the inability of tenants to adequately inspect or repair rental units, the disparity of bargaining power between landlord and tenant, the scarcity of housing in the Commonwealth, and the effect of uninhabitable dwellings on the public health and safety."

Kentucky, however, refused to imply a warranty of habitability in Miles v. Shauntee (1983). The "general rule in effect in Kentucky, is that a tenant takes premises as he finds them.... In the absence of a special agreement to do so, made when the contract is entered into, there is no obligation upon the landlord to repair the premises." Nor did an implied warranty of habitability "arise from local housing or health codes absent an express provision ... in the ordinance or regulation in question."

### 3.   OCCUPIERS OF PREMISES

The traditional rule has been that occupiers of premises, including business occupiers, owe at most a duty of care to those using the premises. This rule has been applied to hoteliers as well. Livingston v. Begay (1982) (carbon monoxide escaping from space heater).

In the landmark case of Becker v. IRM Corp. (1985), California held that a hotel owner could be found strictly liable to a guest who was injured from untempered glass in a shower room door. Said the court: "We are satisfied that the rationale" of strict products liability "requires us to conclude that a landlord engaged in the business of leasing dwellings is strictly liable in tort for injuries resulting from a latent defect in the premises when the defect existed at the time the premises were let to the tenant. It is clear that landlords are part of the 'overall producing and marketing enterprise' that makes housing accommodations available to renters."

It is possible that *Becker* will be restricted to landlord-tenant situations, in which case the decision properly belongs in the preceding subsection. Cf. Hutter v. Badalamenti (1977) (no strict liability for dangerous dance floor in restaurant). The products liability rationale of the case, and the unwillingness of many courts to draw fine distinctions among lessors, bailors, licensors and the like, see Garcia v. Halsett (1970) (laundromat strict liability), make it more likely, however, that the case will be extended to include business premises occupiers generally.

A premises occupier who engages in an abnormally dangerous activity may be strictly liable to others, whether on or off the premises, who are injured by such activity. See State, Dept. of Environmental Protection v. Ventron Corp. (1983) (toxic wastes). There is nothing in this doctrine that requires the defendant actor to be regularly engaged in the dangerous activity, although the cases in fact usually involve such a business actor.

The court in T & E Industries, Inc. v. Safety Light Corp. (1991) held that a purchaser of land could sue a predecessor in title for cleanup costs associated with radium contamination of the land. The predecessor, a radium processor, could be found strictly liable for engaging in an abnormally dangerous activity, the court said.

# I.  CONTRIBUTION AND INDEMNITY

## 1.  IN GENERAL

At the common law, contribution was not allowed between joint tortfeasors, probably on much the same rationale that denied recovery to a plaintiff who was contributorily negligent. Most states now allow contribution, usually by statute. There are two principal bases of apportionment—liability by degree of fault, and liability divided equally according to the number of defendants involved. Typically one who is intentionally at fault is not entitled to contribution. Some states have abolished joint liability, and where this has occurred the need for contribution is obviated.

A related doctrine is that of implied indemnity, where one tortfeasor recovers over in full against another tortfeasor. A common basis for this recovery is where the indemnitee (the one seeking recovery) is free from fault or is only vicariously liable, and the indemnitor is the one actually responsible for the victim's injury.

Indemnity—or more correctly, an action for breach of warranty—is also allowed by a seller against his supplier, e.g., a retailer against his supplying wholesaler, a wholesaler against the manufacturer, and so on up the chain of distribution. The possibility of such actions was one of the reasons given for allowing a direct action by the victim against a product manufacturer, without regard to privity, in order to avoid such a circuity of actions.

Where the indemnitee is found not liable, there is a division of authority as to whether that indemnitee can recover from the indemnitor for its attorneys' fee and other costs incurred in defending the claim. Automatic Time and Control Co. v. ifm Electronics (1991) (denying such recovery); Pullman Standard, Inc. v. Abex Corp. (1985) (allowing such recovery, whether or not the indemnitee is held liable).

An indemnity doctrine developed at common law whereby one "passively" or "secondarily" at fault was permitted to recover over in full against one found "actively" or "primarily" at fault. This doctrine is thought to have evolved to circumvent the harshness of the "no-contribution" rule at common law. The distinction between "active" and "passive" fault has proven elusive and difficult to apply, and for that reason a number of courts, as in Vertecs Corp. v. Reichhold Chem. Co., Inc. (1983), have abolished the doctrine.

Other courts have abolished the indemnity doctrine in general, in favor of one of proportionate recovery based on relative degrees of fault. Dole v. Dow Chem. Co. (1972). Full recovery over can still be permitted here if all the fault lies with one party. See Johns–Manville Sales Corp. v. United States (1985) (indemnity allowable against United States if, with superior knowledge, it forced manufacturer to supply asbestos products according to government specifications).

A federal court held in Casey v. Westinghouse Elevator Co. (1986) that Illinois would allow contribution, rather than indemnity, up the stream of commerce (e.g., by a retailer against a wholesaler); Kyrtatas v. Stop & Shop, Inc. (1988) (contribution, rather than indemnity, between retailer and manufacturer was compelled by products liability statute). It is unclear how these courts would treat a statutory claim for indemnity under the warranty provisions of the UCC, or under the "vouching-in" provision of § 2–607 of the UCC.

If one party expressly agrees to indemnify another, such an agreement will allow full recovery over where the agreement is not against public policy. Such an agreement may be against public policy if for example one party agrees to indemnify another for the latter's own fault.

It is unclear whether an indemnity claim requires parties to be in privity, on the theory that only economic loss is involved. Presumably, by analogy to contribution claims which are allowed although privity often does not exist, there should be no privity requirement in indemnity. The New York appellate court, in Doyle v. Happy Tumbler Wash–O–Mat (1982), held that privity was not necessary in a contribution-indemnity claim based on breach of implied warranty, where the original claim for which indemnity was sought was for personal injuries. But see Hailey v. Schultz (1979) (indemnity claim for personal injuries of original claimant is claim for economic loss of indemnitee requiring privity).

Contribution should be distinguished from comparative fault, although the two are related. In comparative fault, the victim's recovery is reduced by the degree of her own fault or causation. In contribution, a tortfeasor attempts to share liability with another tortfeasor on some basis, including fault. A jurisdiction that applies one of these doctrines may not apply the other, or the basis for apportionment may not be the same where both are applied.

## 2. WHERE GROUNDS OF LIABILITY DIFFER

Where one tortfeasor is held strictly liable and another is held liable in negligence, courts differ as to whether contribution between them is available. Probably the majority rule permits contribution, as in Safeway Stores, Inc. v. Nest–Kart (1978), but the conceptual basis for doing so is not clear. Some courts, as in the related area of comparative fault, allow apportionment in contribution to be made on the basis of comparing relative degrees of fault or of causation.

A similar problem exists where one tortfeasor is intentionally at fault, and another is strictly liable or liable in negligence. Typically the intentional tortfeasor was not entitled to contribution at common law but some courts now allow apportionment in this situation also.

A particularly vexing problem exists where one of the alleged tortfeasors is the victim's employer. This problem arises often in products liability, when a worker is injured by allegedly defective workplace machinery manufactured by a third party.

There are basically three positions taken in this context. One is to allow no contribution by the machine manufacturer against the employer, and in addition to allow the employer a subrogation claim provided by statute against the machine manufacturer for the amount of workers' compensation benefits paid. This rule seems the most unsatisfactory, since it allows a culpable employer to escape without liability. A second position is to eliminate the employer's right of subrogation, and to give the manufacturer credit for the amount of workers' compensation benefits paid. See annot., 43 ALR 4th 849 (1986). A third position, adopted by the *Dole* decision given in the preceding subsection, is to allow the manufacturer to seek contribution based on relative degrees of fault. This position has the effect of indirectly undermining the limited-liability aspect of workers' compensation.

In all events, the employer is never held liable for contribution unless he is at fault. This contrasts with the workplace machine manufacturer's liability, which may be based on strict liability.

## 3.  THE EFFECT OF SETTLEMENTS

The common law was that if the victim settled with one tortfeasor, this settlement automatically released any other cotortfeasor from liability to the victim.  The rule today is often that the settlement does not release a cotortfeasor unless the settlement agreement expressly so provides, although the settlement may insulate the settlor from any claim for contribution.  Some jurisdictions hold that settlement with an indemnitor automatically releases the indemnitee, however.  This rule can be a trap for the unwary where the active-passive indemnity relation resembles a joint tortfeasor situation.

Usually the nonsettling tortfeasor receives a credit on his liability to the victim for any settlement made by a cotortfeasor.  Some jurisdictions determine this credit based on the amount paid in settlement, while others reduce the remaining tortfeasor's liability by the amount of fault attributable to the settling tortfeasor.  The first method tends to encourage settlements more than the second, since in the latter situation the victim runs the risk of releasing part of her claim against the remaining tortfeasor by a settlement that is proportionately less than the percentage of fault attributable to the settlor.

Typically juries are not told about any settlements made in the case.  Brewer v. Payless Stations, Inc. (1982).  A different result obtains, however, where one tortfeasor only conditionally settles, with the understanding that he or she will recover back from the victim all or part of the amount paid in settlement if the victim ultimately recovers from another cotortfeasor. These types of conditional settlements, often called "Mary Carter agreements", are sometimes held invalid as against public policy, Cox v. Kelsey–Hayes Co. (1978), while most courts hold that the substance of the settlement agreement must be made known to the jury in the victim's claim against another cotortfeasor, Hatfield v. Continental Imports, Inc. (1992).

# CHAPTER IV

# FACTORS AFFECTING CHOICE OF REMEDIES, JURISDICTION, AND PROCEDURE

## A. IN GENERAL

Some of the factors discussed in this chapter are more closely associated with one remedy than another. For example, disclaimers, limitations of remedies and notice of breach are often associated with warranty litigation, as is solely economic loss; the reliance element is associated with misrepresentation; the government-contractor defense with design litigation. Such categorizations cannot be neatly maintained, however, since disclaimers, reliance, damages and immunity limitations tend to permeate the law of products liability.

The applicability of other limiting factors tends to vary depending on the remedy asserted. This is particularly true, for example, with conflict of laws questions, disclaimers and statutes of limitations. Such areas are in need of unifying theories.

Still other areas, such as jurisdiction, the effect of statutory compliance, and statutory retrenchments are in a state of flux, probably more so than is true of products law generally. The constant change and developments—some incremental, some substantial and relatively sudden—in products law in general reflect the vitality and growth of this subject.

## B.  RELIANCE

Proof of reliance is expressly required as a condition to recovery for conscious misrepresentation, negligent misrepresentation, and innocent tortious misrepresentation, resulting in personal injury. Rest. 2d of Torts §§ 310, 311, 402B. Moreover, it is a condition to recovery for breach of the implied warranty of fitness, UCC § 2–315. However, in Hebron Pub. School v. U.S. Gypsum (1992) the court said proof of reliance was not required in a case based on breach of the warranty of fitness since the warranty claim was "grounded in tort" and "not in contract."

The express warranty provision, UCC § 2–313, is apparently less demanding in this regard. The Code provides only that the warranty must become a "part of the basis of the bargain." Comment 3 to this section states that "no particular reliance need be shown" in order to "weave [statements] into the fabric of the agreement," and that "any fact which is to take such affirmations, once made, out of the agreement requires clear affirmative proof." In Bernick v. Jurden (1982) (hockey mouthguard—advertised as providing "maximum protection to lips and teeth"—shattered), where the plaintiff's mother bought the product, the court said the "natural tendency" of defendant's express warranty was to "induce purchase", so that "reliance may be inferred." In Cipollone v. Liggett Group, Inc. (1990) (cigarette case) the court said that in order to recover for breach of express warranty the plaintiff must "prove that Mrs. Cipollone had read, seen, or heard the advertisements at issue", and then the defendant would be allowed to show by way of defense that "she did not believe the safety assurances" contained in the advertisements.

The express warranty provision of the UCC, § 2–313(2), states that "an affirmation merely of the value of the goods or a statement purporting to be merely the seller's opinion or commendation of the goods does not create a warranty." It is widely stated that a seller's mere "puffing" does not create a warranty, since the buyer is not entitled to place reliance on such statements. However, puffing is not easy to identify, and opinion may constitute a basis of the bargain where the seller is an alleged expert. Lovington Cattle Feeders, Inc. v. Abbott Labs. (1982) (cattle vaccine).

Comment j to the Rest. 2d of Torts § 402B recognizes that the reliance need not be that of the product user who is injured, but may be that of the purchaser who because of his reliance passes the product on to the user. The comment also recognizes that adequate reliance may exist where the representation induces either the purchase or the use of the product. In the *Bernick* warranty case discussed above, the "reliance" (basis of the bargain) was on the part of plaintiff's mother, in purchasing the product.

A representation may be relevant in determining foreseeable use, as well as reliance. Leichtamer v. American Motors (1981). Even when not relied on, a representation may go to establish the product's intended use and its fitness therefor, Sterner v. U.S. Plywood Champion Paper, Inc. (1975), and to establish foreseeable use, Hiller v. Kawasaki Motors Corp., U.S.A. (1983).

Where the plaintiff is not required to prove reliance, he may nevertheless lose if the evidence shows that he did not either expressly or impliedly rely on the defendant or his product. Erdman v. Johnson Bros. Radio & Telev. Co. (1970). In this situation the issue is closely related to that of causation, and to the affirmative defenses of contributory negligence and assumption of the risk which are also a part of the causation question.

An analogous causation issue concerns the plaintiff's failure to read warnings that are alleged to be inadequate. If the alleged inadequacy is in the content of the warning, the court in E.R. Squibb & Sons, Inc. v. Cox (1985) said the plaintiff who did not read the warning is unable to recover. But if the alleged inadequacy is in the method of communication, the plaintiff may be able to recover even though he did not read the warning that was given. Rhodes v. Interstate Battery System of America, Inc. (1984). Apparently the difference is based on the assumption that a better-communicated warning might have attracted the user's attention and caused him to read it, while fuller content should not be assumed capable of such causal effect.

The underlying basis for requiring proof of some sort of reliance, at least in the case of misrepresentation, is that the misrepresentation creates special expectations regarding product use over and above those presumed to be held by the ordinary consumer. In order to be entitled to such special expectations, the consumer must be aware of and thus rely on the representations in using the product. This analysis breaks down, however, where the representations affirm ordinary expectations, and where the reliance is that of another or where it induces purchase rather than use. Indeed, contractual agreements typically need not be read in order to be binding on the parties. The law of contractual consideration in this regard rests in uneasy tension with the tort doctrine of reliance.

## C. DISCLAIMERS AND LIMITATIONS OF REMEDIES

### 1. IN GENERAL

One of the primary reasons for the modern development of the doctrine of strict tort products liability was to avoid the contractual restrictions on liability available in warranty law. As stated in comment *m* to Rest. 2d of Torts § 402A: "The consumer's cause of action does not depend upon the validity of his contract with the person from whom he acquires the product, and it is not affected by any disclaimer or other agreement, whether it be between the seller and his immediate buyer, or attached to and accompanying the product into the consumer's hands."

The major thrust of strict tort products liability, as set forth in Rest. 2d of Torts § 402A, is to provide compensation to the user or consumer who suffers "physical harm" to himself or to his property from an unreasonably dangerous defective product. It would seem to follow that any restriction of liability would also be ineffective whenever the consumer suffers such damage, but this is not the case. Contractual restrictions for physical harm may be effective in negligence or warranty, even though not in strict tort. No problem is presented to the consumer by this difference as long as she has a strict tort remedy, as is the case in the overwhelming majority of American jurisdictions. Where that remedy is unavailable, however, owing to some defense such as the statute of limitations, or because the court finds the law of strict tort products liability is inapplicable, then a contractual restriction may be effective under negligence or warranty law.

A substantial problem regarding the scope of strict tort products liability concerns the nature of the damage suffered. If physical injury to person is involved, courts will generally allow recovery in strict tort without regard to whether the plaintiff is a lay person or a business person. Where any other type of damage is involved, a considerable division of authority exists as to whether strict tort law applies. This issue implicates the economic loss problem discussed in the next section of this chapter. Some courts apply strict tort for any type of loss if the plaintiff is a consumer, while others believe economic loss should be left exclusively to the law of contracts. All courts, however, will strike down a contractual limitation if it is unconscionable, oppressive, or unfair.

The Uniform Commercial Code distinguishes between disclaimers and limitations of remedies. A disclaimer arises when no remedy is given, UCC § 2–316, while a limitation of remedies exists when the plaintiff is given some remedy which may be different from or less than that otherwise provided by law, UCC § 2–719. The Code attaches different legal effects depending on whether a disclaimer or limitation of remedy is involved, as will be discussed below, while generally tort law draws no such distinction. The term "disclaimer" will be used generically herein to describe both concepts unless otherwise indicated.

## 2.  GENERAL REQUIREMENTS

### a.  Conspicuousness and Clarity

A disclaimer will be invalidated if it is inconspicuous or unclear. A disclaimer on the back of a purchase form, or one hidden away in the small print of a contract, may be ineffective for lack of conspicuousness. Hunt v. Perkins Machinery Co. (1967).

The UCC, § 2–316(2), provides that a disclaimer or modification of the implied warranty of merchantability "must mention merchantability", and "in case of a writing" must be conspicuous as defined in § 1–201(10); and a disclaimer or modification of the implied warranty of fitness "must be by a writing and conspicuous." A clause is defined as "conspicuous" in § 1–201(10) "when it is so written that a reasonable person against whom it is to operate ought to have noticed it. A printed heading in capitals ... is conspicuous. Language in the body of a form is 'conspicuous' if it is in larger or other contrasting type or color." The question of conspicuousness "is for decision by the court." The UCC has no similar express requirement of conspicuousness for a limitation of remedies under § 2–719, although presumably such a requirement can be implied. A disclaimer that is in contrasting type or color might nevertheless be found inconspicuous if hidden away in the body of a contract.

It is common to require that a disclaimer of negligence be in "clear and unequivocal terms" and "contain language which is close enough to express negligence that doubt is removed as to the parties' intent." Stewart & Stevenson Serv., Inc. v. Pickard (1984). The presumption is against the disclaimer of negligence, said the court in DCR Inc.

v. Peak Alarm Co. (1983), and a disclaimer is not achieved "by inference or implication from general language" since if the intent of the parties was to protect the defendant from liability for its "negligent acts, it would have been easy enough to use that very language."

Similarly, in Tyus v. Resta (1984), the court held that a provision in a contract for the purchase of a house was ineffective to disclaim the implied warranty of habitability, where the contract merely stated that the buyer had inspected the premises and that the written contract was the entire agreement between the parties. The warranty of habitability is of such importance, said the court, that it may be limited or disclaimed only by "clear and unambiguous language."

A leading case holding a contractual disclaimer ineffective on grounds of ambiguity is Henningsen v. Bloomfield Motors, Inc. (1960). There the contract provided a limited warranty of repair, "this warranty being expressly in lieu of all other warranties expressed or implied, and all other obligations or liabilities" of the defendant. The court held that this disclaimer was ineffective to disclaim liability for personal injury claims which "are nowhere mentioned." The buyer might well have concluded that the disclaimer applied only to the replacement of defective parts and that she "would not be entitled to a new car" in the event of such a defect.

### b.  Timeliness

A disclaimer must be timely delivered in order to be effective. This means that it must be delivered by the time the agreement has been concluded in order to become part of the contract. Thus, a disclaimer contained in an "owner's manual", delivered after the sale, was held ineffective in Stevens v. Daigle and Hinson Rambler, Inc. (1963). A disclaimer contained in a warranty delivered to the buyer after he signed the contract was held unenforceable in Dorman v. International Harvester Co. (1975). The late delivery of a disclaimer in an instruction manual is ineffective to bind the parties even when the disclaimer is conspicuous and the buyer is a "sophisticated commercial enterprise." Bowdoin v. Showell Growers, Inc. (1987).

While UCC § 2–209 states that an agreement modifying a sales contract needs no additional consideration to be binding, there must nevertheless be an agreement to modify. An acceptance containing different terms from an offer operates as an acceptance with the additional terms being merely proposals for addition to the contract; these proposals do not become part of the contract except between non-objecting merchants, and not even then if the additional terms materially alter the contract. UCC § 2–207. Therefore, the late (post-sale) delivery of a disclaimer would not be binding under UCC §§ 2–207 and 2–209.

## c. Fulfillment of Essential Purpose

UCC § 2–719(2) provides: "Where circumstances cause an exclusive or limited remedy to fail of its essential purpose, remedy may be had as provided in this Act." This provision typically comes into play when the seller limits its liability to repair or replacement of defective parts, and then is unable to make repairs after a reasonable length of time or of attempts to do so, as in Seely v. White Motor Co. (1965). What is a reasonable length of time or a reasonable number of attempts at repair for new automobiles is frequently defined by state motor vehicle warranty legislation ("lemon laws"), see annot., 51 ALR 4th 872 (1986). In Rudd Constr. Equip. Co., Inc. v. Clark Equip. Co. (1984), the court found a failure of essential purpose where the remedy was limited to repair of a defective part which was destroyed in an accident and thus could not be repaired. In Held v. Mitsubishi Aircraft Int'l, Inc. (1987) the court found that a contract limitation to repair or replacement during a limited time period was unenforceable as to latent defects not discoverable within that period. The case involved problems both of failure of purpose under UCC § 2–719 and of a manifestly unreasonable time limitation under UCC § 1–204.

Upon failure of the essential purpose, as noted in § 2–719(2), the buyer is normally relegated to all of his available remedies at law. The *Rudd* court, however, allowed the plaintiff to recover the purchase price of a defective tractor but upheld the limitation as to the exclusion of lost profits. Perhaps this holding is explainable on the ground that the buyer in that case was a sophisticated purchaser, not a lay consumer.

It should be noted that the essential-purpose provision of UCC § 2–719(2) applies by its terms only to limitations of remedies, and not to disclaimers where no remedy at all is provided. The rationale of § 2–719(2) can nevertheless be applied to a disclaimer situation. Indeed, comment 1 to § 2–719 states that "it is of the very essence of a sales contract that at least minimum adequate remedies be available." Where that minimum is lacking in a disclaimer, a failure of essential purpose will commonly be analyzed under the doctrine of conscionability, which is discussed next.

## d. Conscionability

UCC § 2–302 provides that if the court finds a contract or contract clause to be unconscionable, it may refuse to enforce the contract or enforce it without the unconscionable clause. A leading case dealing with unconscionability is Henningsen v. Bloomfield Motors, Inc. (1960). There the court refused to enforce a limited-remedy clause excluding recovery for consequential damages, including personal injuries, because the contract was a standardized form used by virtually the entire automobile industry with the buyer having no "real choice in the matter."

Comment 1 to § 2–302 states that the principle of that section "is one of the prevention of oppression and unfair surprise ... and not of disturbance of allocation of risks because of superior bargaining power." The doctrine of unconscionability has been widely applied, however, to invalidate disclaimers because of inequality of bargaining power.

In Southland Farms, Inc. v. Ciba–Geigy Corp. (1991) the court upheld a disclaimer of liability for consequential damages allegedly resulting from an agricultural chemical. The court said the disclaimer was an "accepted method" of allocating risks in the industry. It noted the "vagaries of nature," and it assumed that if the loss for such damages were shifted to the seller "the cost of the product would be prohibitive."

In Schmaltz v. Nissen (1988), on the other hand, the court held unconscionable a disclaimer in the sale of sorghum seed, noting that the plaintiffs were not in a position to bargain for more favorable contract terms "nor were they able to test the seed before their purchase." A similar result was reached in Schurtz v. BMW of North America, Inc. (1991), involving the sale of an automobile.

The court in Florida Steel Corp. v. Whiting Corp. (1988) rejected defendant's argument that a disclaimer between commercial parties should be upheld. The case involved the sale of an electric furnace that collapsed during use. Noting a division of authority, the court said the disclaimer should be invalidated because the purpose of invalidation was to encourage safety. That purpose applied whether the plaintiff was a consumer or a commercial party.

## 3. AS AFFECTED BY THE CLAIMS ASSERTED

Disclaimers of fraud or deceit are unenforceable. See Epperson v. Roloff (1986) (integration clause in contract for sale of realty does not bar claim for deceit).

A number of courts hold that a disclaimer of liability for negligence is invalid as against public policy. See DCR Inc. v. Peak Alarm Co. (1983). Such disclaimers may be prohibited by statute in certain situations, as for example with regard to landlords or building contractors where the public interest is thought to be predominant. In some cases, as noted in the preceding section, courts hold that a disclaimer of negligence must be clear and unequivocal. See Kerry's Bromeliad Nursery v. Reiling (1990). Courts are more likely to uphold disclaimers of negligence for goods or services not found to be essential. Compare Petry v. Cosmopolitan Spa Intern. (1982) (health spa disclaimer upheld), with Olson v. Molzen (1977) (medical malpractice disclaimer invalidated).

As noted above, the UCC contemplates that a disclaimer of all implied warranty liability is enforceable, § 2–316. If an express warranty is given, or the implied warranties are not disclaimed, but the remedy is limited, then a "[l]imitation of consequential damages for injury to the person in the case of consumer goods is prima facie unconscionable", UCC § 2–719(3). "Consumer goods" are defined in the secured transactions article, UCC § 9–109(1), as goods "used or bought primarily for personal, family or household purposes."

The justification for allowing a disclaimer of all liability, including that for personal injuries, while invalidating a limitation that excludes liability for personal injuries, is, according to Tuttle v. Kelly–Springfield Tire Co. (1978), the prevention of unfair surprise; the buyer should understand an exclusion of all liability, but if some remedy is offered then he reasonably expects that the remedy will include recovery for personal injuries. Whether or not this proposed justification is persuasive, the plaintiff can usually avoid a warranty disclaimer by suing in strict tort when personal injuries are involved. Moreover, a complete disclaimer of liability is likely to be found invalid in warranty, by analogy to the strict tort rule where personal injuries are involved, and by recognition that some minimal remedy is normally a basic requirement of any sales contract.

Some states by statute prohibit the disclaimer or modification of implied warranties where consumer goods are involved. On the other hand, some states by statute remove implied warranty coverage in certain cases as for example with regard to blood and human tissue, or livestock sales.

The Magnuson–Moss Act provides that in the case of a limited warranty, "implied warranties may be limited in duration to the duration of a written warranty of reasonable duration, if such limitation is conscionable and is set forth in clear and unmistakable language and prominently displayed on the face of the warranty." 15 U.S.C. § 2308(b). Presumably such a limitation would be unconscionable under state warranty law, however, where personal injuries involving consumer goods are involved. The federal statute provides that "[n]othing in this chapter shall invalidate or restrict any right or remedy of any consumer under State law or under any other Federal law." 15 U.S.C. § 2311(b)(1).

Courts tend to invalidate disclaimers whose effect is to relieve the seller of an obligation imposed by statute. An "as is" disclaimer in the sale of a used car was held invalid in Mulder v. Casho (1964), because it contravened a statutory duty to inspect the brake system. A disclaimer of liability in a truck rental agreement was invalidated in Hunter v. American Rentals (1962), where a statutory duty of trailer-hitch inspection was violated.

It is widely held that strict products liability in tort cannot be disclaimed where personal injuries are involved. The cases are less clear where the damage is physical injury to property not involving personal injury. Some courts have upheld disclaimers of strict tort for such property damage. See K–Lines, Inc. v. Roberts Motor Co. (1975).

Where no physical injury—either to person or property—is involved, but only economic loss, the cases are sharply divided (as will be seen in § D of this Chapter) as to whether a suit can even be brought in tort. The rationale for not allowing solely economic loss suits in tort is largely to restrict plaintiffs to warranty actions so that disclaimers can be enforced. Of course disclaimers could be enforced as in *K–Lines,* or not enforced where for example there is inequality of bargaining position, without regard to the theory on which the plaintiff sues.

## 4. SCOPE AND EFFECT OF DISCLAIMERS

A disclaimer is effective to bind only those who either directly or indirectly are a party to the agreement. A subcontractor was not bound by a disclaimer of liability between his seller and the manufacturer in Groppel Co., Inc. v. U.S. Gypsum Co. (1981). An employee was not bound by a disclaimer between his employer and the product seller in Velez v. Craine & Clark Lumber Corp. (1973). A disclaimer effective as to a retailer did not release the manufacturer in Clark v. DeLaval Separator Corp. (1981).

In Roberts v. Homelite Div. of Textron, Inc. (1986), however, the court held that an employee, injured by a lawnmower purchased by his corporate employer from the defendant, and his spouse were bound by a disclaimer between the employer and the defendant seller. The fact that the purchaser was a corporation "does not change the fact that in reality plaintiffs are the sole proprietors of that establishment. Plaintiffs are the sole shareholders in the corporation. Also, plaintiffs are responsible as general managers to carry out the day-to-day activities of the business. Those activities include dealing with Homelite and receiving the goods sent by Homelite. In essence, plaintiffs are the corporation."

Comment 1 to the third-party-beneficiary provision of the UCC sales article, § 2–318, states: "To the extent that the contract of sale contains provisions under which warranties are excluded or modified, or remedies for breach are limited, such provisions are equally operative against beneficiaries of warranties under this section." It is doubtful whether this comment would be applied against § 2–318 beneficiaries who had little or nothing to do with the seller, and indeed to do so might constitute a denial of due process.

A disclaimer may be invalid in part but effective as to the remainder. A limitation of remedy to repair, excluding recovery for loss of value, was held invalid in Piper Accep. Corp. v. Barton (1987) for failure of essential purpose, but the exclusion of recovery of consequential damages was upheld as conscionable. Accord, Rudd Const. Equip. Co., Inc. v. Clark Equip. Co. (1984) (lost value exclusion invalid, but exclusion of lost profits upheld). Presumably an exclusion of personal injuries could be invalidated, with the remainder of the disclaimer upheld. However, lost wages are an endemic part of a personal injury claim, and probably could not be conscionably excluded. The question of the scope of a disclaimer should be compared with the scope-of-damage issue in the economic loss cases discussed in the next section.

## D. RECOVERY OF SOLELY ECONOMIC LOSS

### 1. THE RULE AND ITS RATIONALE

Many courts hold that a plaintiff cannot recover in tort—either in negligence or in strict liability—when he or she has suffered solely economic loss from a defective product. This rule is often applied whether or not there is privity between the plaintiff and defendant, and whether or not the plaintiff is a business person or a lay person.

The rationales for the rule restricting recovery to warranty for solely economic loss were stated in Seely v. White Motor Co. (1965), which is the case most often cited as authority for the rule. There the court held that a plaintiff could not sue a remote manufacturer (one with whom the plaintiff was not in privity) in strict tort for solely economic loss, since if such an action could be brought the "manufacturer would be liable for damages of unknown and unlimited scope." Moreover, said the court, liability in such an action could not be disclaimed, "for one purpose of strict liability in tort is to prevent a manufacturer from defining the scope of his responsibility for harm caused by his products."

The first rationale of *Seely* (the scope of liability) is dubious. Products recovery, whether in tort or warranty, is limited to foreseeable damages.

The important rationale seems to be the second one—the ability to disclaim. As noted in the preceding section, some courts do determine the validity of a disclaimer based on the theory on which the suit is brought. Negligence should not be disclaimable, for example if such a disclaimer is against public policy. Putting aside negligence, and claims for personal injuries, the issue of disclaimability whether in tort or in warranty should normally turn on questions of conscionability and equality of bargaining position.

If the plaintiff is in an inferior bargaining position, then any disclaimer, whether actual or theoretical, should be ineffective. In that event, the plaintiff should be able to recover whether the suit is brought in tort or warranty, and whether or not the parties are in privity. In determining if such recovery should be allowed, questions of bargaining equality could be decided by looking primarily at the status of the parties.

If on the other hand the parties are equal bargainers, then privity may be required so they can in fact bargain, and recovery denied if there is no privity. When the parties are equal bargainers in privity, a disclaimer should be generally effective to disclaim both warranty and tort liability. If they did not negotiate a disclaimer, then the plaintiff should be left to her remedies at law including tort and warranty.

Where the parties are equal bargainers and they draft a disclaimer, it may well be unenforceable as drawn for example because of the presence of negligence, fraud, lack of clarity, inconspicuousness, or untimeliness. These are conscionability kinds of issues that go to the validity of the contractual agreement, rather than to the status of the parties. Thus, equality of bargaining position in terms of status would require that the parties be in privity so they could negotiate, but it would not ensure that the negotiation would be enforceable.

Where personal injuries are involved, the policy of safety promotion may invalidate disclaimers without regard to the status of the parties or the fairness of the contract. This same policy may apply to invalidate disclaimers where pure economic loss is involved, if the defective condition of the product is dangerous but fortuitously does not cause personal injury.

There is some indication that solely economic loss is not commercially insurable under the typical products liability policy, which requires proof of an "occurrence" as the basis for indemnity. Such loss is, however, self-insurable. Assuming the unavailability of insurance, this factor argues in favor of requiring privity so as to give the seller an opportunity to disclaim such uninsured exposure if the status of the parties is equal, the agreement is fair, and no public policy (such as promotion of safety) is violated.

## 2. DEFINITIONS OF SOLELY ECONOMIC LOSS

Economic loss is typically defined as loss in value, loss of use, cost of replacement, lost profits, and damage to business reputation, where no sudden, physical accident is involved. See Fordyce Concrete, Inc. v. Mack Trucks, Inc. (1982). Where there is an accident, a tort action can normally be maintained without privity to recover all damages suffered, including economic losses. See LeSueur Creamery, Inc. v. Haskon, Inc. (1981). The *Fordyce* case, above, apparently would allow a tort claim for physical damage to property, however, while denying such a claim for accompanying economic losses. Arguably—by analogy to the disclaimer cases in the preceding section, where a disclaimer can be good for some purposes although not for others—an action in warranty with privity could be required for economic losses even when physical injury is involved. The courts, however, do not usually split the cause of action for purposes of applying the economic loss rule, but instead treat the economic loss as parasitic to physical damage when the latter is present.

A court may require plaintiff's physical damage to be substantial before a tort action can be brought. This requirement is illustrated in Florida Power & Light Co. v. McGraw Edison Co. (1988). The rule that the court applied there required either that there be personal injury to the plaintiff, or physical damage to property other than the defective product itself, in order for a suit in tort to lie. The defective product, a power station transformer, exploded causing damage to itself, and also to other property in plaintiff's power station surrounding the transformer. The court said this other-property damage was minimal, and not sufficient to justify recovery in tort.

It is not always easy to determine from the cases what constitutes an accident so as to permit a suit in tort. The cases usually require that the defective product cause "sudden, calamitous damage" in order for tort law to apply. Such damage was found in United Air Lines, Inc. v. CEI Industries (1986), where a defective roof suddenly collapsed, even though the collapse was the result of gradual deterioration.

In Jones & Laughlin Steel Corp. v. Johns–Manville Sales Corp. (1980), the court found no accident when a defective roof "began to blister, wrinkle, and crack," where such cracks "permitted water to enter the steel mill, which in turn damaged some of the steel products under construction and caused electrical outages," and where "portions of the asbestos fell and Fesco Board began to tear away from the deck of the roof" as a result of the defect. On the other hand, the court in Board of Education of City of Chicago v. A, C & S, Inc. (1989) found that damage resulting from the removal of asbestos from plaintiff's school buildings constituted physical damage, so that an action in tort could be maintained for the cost of removal.

A number of courts hold that damage only to the defective product itself, even where that damage occurs as the result of a sudden, violent accident, is economic loss for which no tort claim will lie. Oklahoma Gas & Electric Co. v. McGraw–Edison Co. (1992). The rationale for this rule is that such damage is simply a loss to the purchaser of the benefit of her bargain, and should therefore be governed by the law of warranty. The rule is followed in federal admiralty cases. East River S.S. Corp. v. Transamerica Delaval, Inc. (1986). Other courts treat damage to the property itself, at least where it occurs as the result of an accident, as physical injury giving rise to a claim in tort.

Some courts do not require an accident to invoke the tort doctrine. They hold it sufficient to allow recovery in tort if the defective product poses a health hazard. 80 South Eighth Street Ltd. v. Carey–Canada, Inc. (1992) (asbestos fireproofing material). The reasoning here is that tort law is designed to deter risky conduct, and that deterrence can be effected whether liability for such conduct is imposed before or after an accident occurs.

There is a division of authority as to whether an indemnity claim is one for economic loss when the indemnitee seeks recovery from the indemnitor for damages paid on a claim for personal injuries. Compare Hailey v. Schultz (1979) (economic loss) with Doyle v. Happy Tumbler Wash–O–Mat, Inc. (1982) (since the injured victim would have a claim in strict tort, the indemnitee's claim "is not for consequential economic loss").

It is unclear whether a claim for emotional distress not involving physical injury would be treated as economic loss. Thomas v. Olin Mathieson Chem. Corp. (1967) (loss of honor and prestige) apparently holds without discussion that it would be economic loss. But compare Foley v. Polaroid Corp. (1980) (intentional infliction of emotional distress), where mental distress is treated as personal injury compensable as such under workers' compensation.

### 3. EXCEPTIONS TO THE RULE

Some courts make no distinction between solely economic loss and physical injury, and allow recovery in tort in either case. In allowing the consumer to bring an action in strict tort for solely economic loss against the manufacturer of a defective mobile home, the court in Thompson v. Nebraska Mobile Homes Corp. (1982) gave these reasons for doing so:

> Warranties are easily disclaimed. Negligence is difficult, if not impossible, to prove. The consumer does not generally have large damages to

attract the attention of lawyers who must handle these cases on a contingent fee. We feel that the consumer should be protected by affording a legal remedy which causes the manufacturer to bear the costs of its own defective products.

Santor v. A & M Karaghensian, Inc. (1965) is often cited as the leading case allowing recovery in strict tort for solely economic loss against the remote manufacturer of a defective product. This case was modified in Spring Motors Distributors, Inc. v. Ford Motor Co. (1985) to require the commercial plaintiff to bring an action for solely economic loss in warranty, although privity was not required in such a case. The rationale of the case is that commercial parties can bargain for disclaimers, presumably through an intermediary in the absence of privity, and the warranty requirement of notice of breach can also reasonably be imposed. The *Spring Motors* holding permitting recovery in implied warranty without privity rather than in tort for solely economic loss has been applied by some courts without regard to the plaintiff's status, as in Morrow v. New Moon Homes, Inc. (1976).

Recovery in negligence without privity for pure economic loss is allowed by some courts, e.g., Berg v. General Motors Corp. (1976). This rule has been widely followed in admiralty, Miller Industries v. Caterpillar Tractor Co. (1984) but it was rejected as the federal admiralty rule in East River Steamship Corp. v. Transamerica Delaval, Inc. (1986).

Recovery of solely economic loss without privity based on breach of express warranty is often allowed, as in Randy Knitwear v. American Cyanamid Co. (1962). Indeed, such recovery was allowed in the landmark case of Seely v. White Motor Co. (1965), which established the rule denying recovery in tort for solely economic loss.

The *Santor* case, supra, which allowed recovery in strict tort for economic loss, also noted that implicit in a product's presence on the market is a representation that the product is "suitable for the general purposes for which it is sold and for which such goods are generally appropriate." Using this approach would enable courts to extend the *Seely* holding to products cases in general.

An action for pure economic loss may be brought in tort based on fraudulent misrepresentation. First Nat. Bank v. Brooks Farms (1991). It would seem that a similar action could be brought for negligent misrepresentation, although there is authority to the contrary, Board of Education of City of Chicago v. A, C & S, Inc. (1989).

In Ales–Peratis Foods Intern., Inc. v. American Can Co. (1985), the court held that the plaintiff could recover in negligence against a can manufacturer for the value of defective cans and a resulting loss of a contract, where the defendant knew for whom the cans were intended. This suit resembles a claim for breach of the implied warranty of fitness for a particular purpose, which bears a close likeness to an action for breach of express warranty where privity is not required.

The same economic loss question that arises in products cases also arises in realty transactions. There is a division of authority as to whether a real estate purchaser can sue the original builder in tort, or without privity of contract, for pure economic loss. See Lempke v. Dagenais (1988). The issue is of considerable importance in realty cases, since damages suffered in this context often involve only economic loss rather than physical injury.

Some courts have allowed products liability recovery in tort based on the breach of a post-sale duty to warn. In allowing such recovery the court said in Miller Industries v. Caterpillar Tractor Co. (1984): "Whatever the merits of adopting a rule that views defects in a product as part of the parties' bargain and thus within the law of sales, it is much less tenable to presume that the buyer has bargained away the manufacturer's obligation to warn of defects that later come to the manufacturer's attention." This rule has been rejected where denial of recovery in tort for pure economic loss is based on the assumption that recovery for pure economic loss, whether or not fault is present, "is better adjusted by contract rules than by tort principles." Continental Ins. Co. v. Page Engineering Co. (1989).

The numerous exceptions to the rule barring recovery for pure economic loss, and the conceptual difficulties encountered in defining what is pure economic loss, suggest that the rule itself is an unsatisfactory one. There may be a trend to allow recovery on the basis of the status of the parties, with recovery being allowed in tort where the plaintiff is a lay person as opposed to a business person. In addition, there appears to be a trend to allow recovery in tort where the product defect poses a safety hazard, or where the defendant is at fault. These trends further the goals of tort law, while leaving to warranty those situations where contractual remedies including the ability to disclaim seem appropriate.

## E.  NOTICE OF BREACH

The Uniform Commercial Code, § 2–607(3)(a), provides:

> (3) Where a tender has been accepted

> (a) the buyer must within a reasonable time after he discovers or should have discovered any breach notify the seller of breach or be barred from any remedy.

One of the primary reasons for the development of the doctrine of strict tort in products liability was to avoid the warranty requirement of notice of breach, as well as the privity and disclaimer aspects of warranty law. Indeed, the landmark case of Greenman v. Yuba Power Products, Inc. (1962) fashioned the doctrine of strict tort for products liability to eliminate the issue of adequacy of notice present in that case. The notice requirement, said the *Greenman* court,

> is not an appropriate one for the court to adopt in actions by injured consumers against manufacturers with whom they have not dealt. "As between the immediate parties to the sale [the notice requirement] is a sound commercial rule, designed to protect the seller against unduly delayed claims for damages. As applied to personal injuries, and notice to a remote seller, it becomes a booby-trap for the unwary. The injured consumer is seldom steeped in the business practice which justifies the rule," [James, Product Liability, 34 Texas L. Rev. 44, 192, 197] and at least until he has had legal advice it will not occur to him to give notice to one with whom he has had no dealings.

The purpose of the notice requirement is to enable the defendant to have early knowledge of a potential claim so the defendant can investigate and attempt settlement. It differs from the vouching-in procedure of UCC § 2–607(5)(a), which permits a buyer who is sued for breach of warranty to give his seller notice of the claim and an opportunity to come in and defend, so the seller will be bound by determinations of fact common to the claim against the buyer and the buyer's claim against the seller. It also differs from a statute of limitations, which is designed to put claims to rest after a specified period of time, regardless of whether the defendant knows or does not know of the claim.

The notice requirement is given a practical, rather than a technical, application. In Prutch v. Ford Motor Co. (1980), notice to the dealer was held sufficient notice for the manufacturer where the dealer in turn promptly advised the manufacturer who investigated the problem. Actual notice, rather than formal notice from the plaintiff, is all that is required. The length of time within which notice must be given will depend on the circumstances, see Castro v. Stanley Works (1989) (20–month delay too long). The content of the notice "need merely be sufficient to let the seller know that the transaction is ... troublesome." Comment 4 to § 2–607.

Section 2–607(3)(a) provides that "the buyer" must give notice of breach. Comment 5 to the section states that this notice requirement is intended to apply to third-party beneficiaries under § 2–318 as well. The court in Frericks v. General Motors Corp. (1976) refused to apply the notice requirement to a non-buyer plaintiff, however, noting that while "the official comments are a valuable aid to construction, they have not been enacted by the Legislature, and 'the plain language of the statute cannot be varied by reference to the comments'".

The notice section by its terms bars the plaintiff from "any remedy" if timely notice is not given. As already noted, the section has been held inapplicable to an action in strict tort, and apparently it has not been applied to a negligence suit in products liability. The court in Begley v. Jeep Corp. (1980) applied it, however, to a breach of warranty action in the nature of indemnity by a manufacturer against a component supplier. Contra, Daugherty v. Farmers Co-op. Ass'n (1989) (notice requirement inapplicable to indemnity claim). In Spring Motors Distributors, Inc. v. Ford Motor Co. (1985), the court applied the notice requirement to a commercial plaintiff against a remote manufacturer for solely economic loss, since the court held that such a claim was restricted to warranty. In Pollard v. Saxe & Yolles Dev. Co. (1974), the court applied the notice section to an action by purchasers against the builder-vendors of apartment buildings for breach of the implied warranty of fitness. While acknowledging that the sales article of the UCC applied only to the sale of goods, it nevertheless considered the reasons for the notice requirement to be "as applicable to builders and sellers of new construction as to manufacturers and dealers of chattels."

## F. WRONGFUL DEATH

A wrongful death action is typically a creature of statute, rather than a common law cause of action. Most of the statutes speak in terms of an action for death resulting from a crime, negligence, carelessness, wrongful act, or default of another. Courts have had no difficulty in allowing a tort action based on such statutes, whether brought for reck-lessness, negligence, or strict liability. A few courts have held, however, that such statutes were not intended to authorize an action for breach of warranty.

The better reasoned decisions, and the majority of courts, allow a wrongful death action to be brought in warranty, as well as in tort. They find that a breach of warranty "may be likewise a wrongful act." Schnabl v. Ford Motor Co. (1972). The court in Commercial Truck & Trailer Sales v. McCampbell (1979) said: "We are unwilling to construe the Code [the UCC] as narrowly as the petitioners contend, so as to permit an action for personal injuries as consequential damages for breach of a warranty, but to preclude one when those injuries result in death prior to suit."

If strict tort involves a culpable act for purposes of wrongful death statutes, as apparently all courts hold, then there is no justification for failing to find a culpable act in strict liability for breach of warranty as well. As the court said in Guarino v. Mine Safety Appl. Co. (1969), in extending the rescue doctrine to an action for breach of warran-ty: "A breach of warranty and an act of negligence are each clearly wrongful acts." In eliminating the privity requirement, the court in Madouros v. Kansas City Coca–Cola Bottling Co. (1936) said: "If privity of contract is required, then, under the situation of modern merchandise in such matters, privity of contract exists in the consciousness and understanding of all right-thinking persons." Similarly, if culpability is required in a breach of warranty action for wrongful death, then it should exist "in the consciousness and understanding of all right-thinking persons."

# G.  PROCEDURAL CONSIDERATIONS
## 1.  JURISDICTION

### a.  Statutory Causes of Action

As discussed in § C of Chapter II above, a statute may provide the basis for a cause of action, either expressly or by implication. Thus in Valley Datsun v. Martinez (1979) the court held that the state's consumer protection statute created a right to treble damages plus attorney's fees where the defendant breached an express warranty in the sale of a vehicle. Defendant contended its statement that the vehicle was in "excellent condition" was mere "dealer's talk", but the court said that "knowledge of the seller, in conjunction with the buyer's relative ignorance, operates to make the slightest diversion from mere praise into representations of fact."

Under the Swine Flu Act, 42 U.S.C. §§ 247b(j)–247b(1) (1976), the United States assumed liability for all swine flu vaccine program participants, including vaccine manufacturers and medical personnel. The liability is grounded on any theory available in the state where the vaccine is given.

The court in Swenson v. Emerson Elec. Co. (1985) found that "Congress created a private right of action for damages in certain instances, for persons injured 'by reason of any knowing (including wilful) violation of a consumer product safety rule, or any other rule or order issued by the [Consumer Product Safety] Commission.' 15 U.S.C. § 2072(a) (1982)." This remedy is "in addition to and not in lieu of any other remedies provided by common law or under Federal or State law. Id. § 2072(c).

The United States Supreme Court by a 5–4 vote held in Merrell Dow Pharmaceuticals, Inc. v. Thompson (1986) that an alleged violation of the Federal Food, Drug, and Cosmetic Act (FDCA), 21 U.S.C. § 301 et seq. (1982 ed., Supp. II), did not give rise to federal-question jurisdiction. Both parties agreed, and the Court assumed for "purposes of our decision", that a federal cause of action was not created by the FDCA because: 1) plaintiff was not part the class for whose special benefit the statute was passed, 2) there was no apparent Congressional intent to provide a private cause of action, 3) such a cause of action would not further the underlying purposes of the legislative scheme, and 4) the cause of action was one traditionally relegated to state law.

The majority said in order for federal question jurisdiction to be created, the federal law "must be in the forefront of the case and not collateral, peripheral or remote." It found that plaintiff's argument of the need for uniform interpretation of the FDCA went more to the question of whether state court jurisdiction should be preempted than to federal question jurisdiction, and in any event "this Court retains power to review the decision of a federal issue in a state cause of action."

Using the four-part test established by the Supreme Court in Cort v. Ash (1975), the court in Sparks v. Metalcraft, Inc. (1987) found that Congress did not intend to create an implied right of action under the Federal Hazardous Substances Act. First, plaintiff was "not one of the class for whose *especial* benefit the statute was enacted"; second, the statutory emphasis was "preventive, not remedial"; third, a private right of action would be inconsistent with the legislative scheme, which was to provide a "coordinated regulatory program" whose function would be undermined by "multiple and unconstrained private suits"; and finally, products liability claims "are traditionally the concern of state law" rather than of federal suits.

## b.  Minimum Contacts of the Defendant

The due process clause of the United States Constitution requires that a defendant have minimum contacts with a forum before it can be subjected to the personal jurisdiction of that forum. Thus in World–Wide Volkswagen Corp. v. Woodson (1980) plaintiffs were severely injured in an automobile accident while travelling through Oklahoma.  Alleging a defective design of the gas tank which caused the tank to rupture and catch fire in the accident, they brought suit in Oklahoma against the manufacturer, the importer, the regional distributor, and the retailer.  The distributor and retailer appealed alleging lack of personal jurisdiction.

Reversing the Oklahoma Supreme Court, the United States Supreme Court held that these two defendant-appellants were not subject to service of process in Oklahoma because they had not purposefully availed themselves "of the privilege of conducting business in the forum state."  They had made no efforts "to serve directly or indirectly" the Oklahoma market.  The retailer sold only in Massena, N.Y., and the wholesaler's market was limited to New York, New Jersey and Connecticut. The fact that it was "foreseeable" that cars might be purchased by those who would take them to Oklahoma was not enough to give jurisdiction, since mere "unilateral activity of those who claim some relationship with a nonresident defendant cannot satisfy the requirement of contact with the forum state."  The court did not have before it the question of whether the manufacturer and the importer were properly subject to service of process in Oklahoma.

The courts divide on what constitutes an attempt to serve a market "directly or indirectly" or to "purposely avail" oneself of the privilege of conducting business in a forum state.  The outcome may be related to the extent of the defendant's activities as a whole.

The deliberate but indirect export of amino acid L-tryptophan by a foreign manufacturer into the United States justified long-arm jurisdiction for resulting personal injuries from the acid, the court held in DeMoss v. City Market, Inc. (1991). The acid was shipped in large quantities through an American wholly-owned subsidiary, and a single bulk shipment was made to Utah where the injury occurred. Similarly, in State ex rel. Hydraulic Servocontrols Corp. v. Dale (1982) the court held that a New York manufacturer of an airplane component part could be required to defend a suit for an airplane crash in Oregon allegedly resulting from a defect in the part. Although the defendant did not do business or have an office in Oregon, it "sold a product with the intention of deriving economic benefit from a national market."

In Vioski v. Calaveras Asbestos Ltd. (1991), on the other hand, a foreign supplier who sold asbestos to a California purchaser, with the expectation that the product would only be used in that state, could not be sued in Illinois for injuries allegedly caused by the product in the latter state. The product was resold to an Illinois purchaser without notice to the defendant.

A plurality of four held in Asahi Metal Industry Co., Ltd. v. Superior Court of California (1987) that a foreign manufacturer did not purposefully avail itself of an American market in California merely because it was foreseeable that its product would be sold in that jurisdiction. In that case the plaintiff was severely injured, and his wife killed, in a motorcycle accident allegedly caused by a tire tube containing a defective valve assembly that precipitated a blowout and crash. Plaintiff sued the Taiwanese manufacturer of the tube, and the manufacturer filed a third-party complaint seeking indemnity from Asahi, a Japanese corporation and the component manufacturer of the tube's valve assembly. The underlying action was settled, leaving on appeal only the question of personal jurisdiction of the defendant in the indemnity claim.

The plurality found that while a few of Asahi's valves were sold in California, and that while such sales were foreseeable, foreseeability was an insufficient basis for jurisdiction where the defendant took no action "purposefully directed toward the forum state." It did not do business in California, had "no office, agents, employees, or property" in that state, did not advertise there, or "create, control or employ the distribution system" that brought the valves to California, and did not design its product "in anticipation of sales in California."

A majority of five rejected this rationale as the basis for the decision. They held instead that a citizen of a foreign nation, in a dispute with a citizen of another foreign nation arising out of a Taiwanese transaction, could not be required "to traverse the distance" from its home to California and subject itself "to a foreign nation's judicial system"; "California's legitimate interests in the dispute have considerably diminished" as a result of the settlement of the underlying claim, and the indemnitee "has not demonstrated that it is more convenient for it to litigate its indemnification claim against Asahi in California rather than in Taiwan or Japan." Three of the plurality concurred in this alternative basis for the decision. The alternative basis, representing the position of the majority of the court, is obviously considerably more restricted than that of the plurality, and leaves open the question of what constitutes minimum contacts where the defendant is an American, as opposed to a foreign, manufacturer.

### c.   Class Actions and Multi–District Litigation

Considerable interest has developed regarding the use of class actions as a means of handling mass tort litigation—situations involving such products as Agent Orange, asbestos, Bendectin, Dalkon Shield, formaldehyde insulation, and DES, where the same product may cause hundreds and thousands of injuries. Looming on the horizon also is the possibility of mass tort litigation for injuries arising out of toxic landfills and nuclear waste disposals. Heretofore the class action has been thought inappropriate for mass tort claims, owing to the substantially varying individual questions affecting liability and damages. In order to meet a perceived problem of major court congestion from such claims, however, this conclusion of inappropriateness is being reconsidered and altered.

Fed. R. Civ. Proc. 23, which provides a model adopted by many states, sets forth four types of class actions that may be certified on motion of either plaintiff or defendant. They are: 1) where there is a risk of inconsistent or varying adjudications; 2) where adjudication of some claims will as a practical matter be dispositive of the claims of others not a party to the litigation; 3) where the defendant has acted or refused to act on grounds generally applicable to a class, making final injunctive or declaratory relief appropriate; and 4) where questions of fact or law common to the members of the class predominate over questions affecting only individual members. The fourth category is the one most widely thought suitable for mass tort litigation.

All four types of classes require a showing that the class is so numerous that joinder is impractical, that there are common questions of law or fact, that the representative claims are typical, and that the representative parties will fairly protect the interests of the class. The first three types of classes are called "mandatory", in that every member is bound by the judgment. The fourth category is optional, in that any member can on notice request exclusion from the class. The fourth category additionally requires not only that there be common questions of law or fact, but that these questions predominate over individual issues; and that the class action be superior in fairness and efficiency to other available methods of adjudication.

A nationwide class action would arguably provide the greatest efficiency, and such a class was certified in the case of In re School Asbestos Litigation (1986), to determine liability for the costs of removing asbestos insulation from public schools. This suit was the opt-out (fourth) type of class suit. Major problems of personal jurisdiction arise, however, where a mandatory nationwide class is certified. The United States Supreme Court in Phillips Petroleum Co. v. Shutts (1985) held that plaintiffs lacking minimum contacts with the forum cannot be bound by a class action judgment unless they are given the opportunity to opt out of the class.

The federal 4th Circuit certified a class action against an IUD manufacturer, In re A.H. Robins Co. (1989). Apparently the class was intended to be mandatory. But in Waldron v. Raymark Industries, Inc. (1989) the court refused to certify a mandatory class action for all present and future asbestos claims. Certification would violate the constitutional rights of those having insufficient contacts with the forum, the court said. In addition, the suit would require enjoining state actions in violation of the Anti–Injunction Act, 28 U.S.C. § 2283, which prohibits a federal court from enjoining state court proceedings except where expressly authorized by Congress "or where necessary in aid of [the federal court's] jurisdiction or to protect or effectuate its judgment."

In a federal diversity case, diversity between only the representative party and opposing defendants is required, Supreme Tribe of Ben–Hur v. Cauble (1921). But the dollar jurisdictional amount must be met for each member of the plaintiff class. Zahn v. International Paper Co. (1973).

The problem of personal jurisdiction for multistate litigation can perhaps be met in federal courts by use of the multi-district litigation device, 28 U.S.C. § 1407. This statute provides for the transfer of pending similar litigation in different districts to a single district for purposes of resolving pretrial matters. Such a transfer was effected for approximately 30,000 asbestos cases from 87 federal districts, to be tried under Weiner, J., Pa. Docket # 875 (CCH Prod. Liab. Newsl. No. 734, 12 Aug. 1991).

The Texas federal district court in Jenkins v. Raymark Indus., Inc. (1985), certified an optional class of asbestos cases from its district for purposes of making limited determinations of the state-of-the-art defense and the amount of punitive damages, if any, to be imposed in toto. The court contemplated that there would then be mini-trials on the issues of individual liability and damages.

## 2.  INCONSISTENT VERDICTS AND ERRONEOUS INSTRUCTIONS

The court in Gumbs v. International Harvester, Inc. (1983) held that Rest. 2d of Torts § 402A and the warranty of merchantability are coextensive. A special verdict finding defendant's product was not defective and unreasonably dangerous, but that the sale breached the manufacturer's warranty of merchantability, was therefore irreconcilably inconsistent requiring a new trial. In Awedian v. Theodore Efron Mfg. Co. (1976), on the other hand, the court held that a special verdict finding the manufacturer negligent but not guilty of a breach of implied warranty was not inconsistent, apparently because it concluded that proof of negligence does not require proof of a defect. These varying results reflect differing approaches to the issue of overlapping theories of recovery, discussed above in Chapter II. F.

In Clark v. Seagrave Fire Apparatus, Inc. (1988) the court held a verdict in a design case was not inconsistent where the jury found no negligence but did find a breach of the warranty of fitness. This holding seems correct, since a fitness warranty creates expectations over and above those normally present in a negligence claim.

Some courts, as in Elk Corp. of Ark. v. Jackson (1987), hold that if a case is submitted to a jury on a good count (here, negligence) and another count not supported by the evidence (strict liability in this case), then a general verdict for the plaintiff must be reversed and remanded for a new trial. This was the issue raised in Greenman v. Yuba Power Products, Inc. (1963), where the case was submitted to the jury on negligence and breach of warranty but the defendant asserted that inadequate notice was given to support the latter count. The court circumvented the issue by holding that notice of breach was not required in a warranty action (which it recast in terms of strict tort liability), where a consumer sues a remote manufacturer for personal injuries.

Not all jurisdictions follow the rule of *Elk* and *Greenman* in this regard. Tenn. Code Ann. § 20–9–502, for example, provides: "If any counts in a declaration are good, a verdict for entire damages shall be applied to such good counts." This statute has been used not only where there was insufficient evidence to support a count, but also where there were improper instructions that could not have affected all counts. A similar rule is followed by judicial decision in Connecticut. Nichols v. Coppola Motors, Inc. (1979).

## 3.  RES JUDICATA

Estoppel by judgment precludes relitigation of the same cause of action that has been previously litigated to a final judgment between the same parties or their privies. Issue preclusion, or collateral estoppel, precludes relitigation of an issue that has been finally determined in prior litigation between the same parties or their privies—or relitigation of an issue by one party where that issue has been finally determined against that party in previous litigation, when mutuality of parties is not required.

In the case of In re Moorenovich (1986), the court held that plaintiffs could bring an action to recover damages for fear of contracting cancer in the future from prior exposure to asbestos, although the plaintiffs had not yet contracted cancer or suffered any other physical injury as a result of such exposure. "Any such recovery", the court said, "would be for *present* damages, and we do not believe that a plaintiff's cause of action for cancer, should it ultimately develop, would be necessarily foreclosed by *res judicata* under our ruling."

Non-mutual collateral estoppel—where the parties are not the same in successive suits—is of two kinds, defensive and offensive. Non-mutual defensive collateral estoppel arises where the plaintiff has litigated and lost an issue in a prior suit, and a *different defendant* in a later suit attempts to bar the plaintiff from relitigating that issue. Non-mutual offensive collateral estoppel arises when the defendant has litigated and lost an issue in a prior suit, and a *different plaintiff* in a later suit attempts to bar the defendant from relitigating that issue.

Non-mutual defensive collateral estoppel is not uncommon. See, e.g., West v. Kawasaki Motors Mfg. Corp. (1992) (finding of no defect in suit against wholesaler estops plaintiff from relitigating that issue in a subsequent suit against the manufacturer). Courts are reluctant to permit the use of non-mutual offensive collateral estoppel, however. See McAdoo v. Dallas Corp. (1991). Perhaps this reluctance is owing to the fact that the plaintiff is generally thought to have more incentive than the defendant to litigate an issue fully in the first suit, so she can fairly be barred from relitigating that issue in a later suit. A defendant, moreover, can be sued by numerous plaintiffs who arguably should not be able to profit by repeated efforts to bind a single defendant collaterally on an issue.

## 4. CHOICE OF LAW

A federal court sitting in diversity jurisdiction, under the *Erie* doctrine, Erie Railroad Co. v. Tompkins (1938), must apply the choice of law or conflict of law rules of the forum state. Klaxon Co. v. Stentor Elec. Mfg. Co. (1941). Choice of law issues must be distinguished, however, from questions of procedure. If a federal court determines that an issue is procedural under *Erie,* then that court never reaches the question of how the forum state court would treat the same issue for conflict of law purposes. Instead, it applies in own procedural rule.

A state will apply its own procedural rules, even though it might apply the substantive law of another jurisdiction provided that law does not conflict with the state's public policy.  A procedural rule for state law purposes may nevertheless be substantive under *Erie* for federal diversity jurisdiction purposes.

But if a federal court setting in diversity finds its own rule to be procedural for purposes of *Erie*, then it will apply its rule instead of that of the forum state.  This is true whether the state considers its rule to be procedural or substantive for choice of law purposes.  Federal procedural rules, for purposes of *Erie*, are typically those governed by the federal rules of procedure and the federal rules of evidence.

Where there is a transfer of venue from one federal court to another, the United States Supreme Court in Van Dusen v. Barrack (1964) held that under the federal change-of-venue statute, 28 U.S.C. § 1404, the transferee court must apply the conflict rules of the transferor.  This holding may also apply to a multi-district-litigation transfer under 28 U.S.C. § 1407.

A federal court sitting in diversity is allowed some latitude in determining the choice of law rules of the forum state.  Saloomey v. Jeppesen & Co. (1983) was a case brought in the Connecticut federal district court for the wrongful death of Connecticut residents killed in a plane crash in West Virginia allegedly owing to faulty navigational maps supplied by the defendant, a Colorado corporation.  Although Connecticut used the lex loci delicti rule in determining choice of law for automobile accidents—which rule would have dictated the choice of West Virginia law here—the court nevertheless concluded that Connecticut would apply Colorado law. It did so because of the "judicial trend" toward adoption of the "most significant relationship" test of Rest. 2d Conflict of Laws § 145 (1971), which the court assumed Connecticut would follow in a case such as this.

The United States Supreme Court in Phillips Petroleum Co. v. Shutts (1985) placed due process limitations on the power of a state to make choice-of-law decisions. There, in a class action brought by gas company investors to recover interest on royalties that accrued pending final administrative approval of a gas price increase, the court held that the Kansas state court could not apply its own law to all the claims in the case. "[O]ver 99% of the gas leases and some 97% of the plaintiffs in the case had no apparent connection to the State of Kansas except for this lawsuit." In order to apply its own law, "Kansas must have a 'significant contact or aggregation of contacts' to the claims asserted by each member of the plaintiff class, contacts 'creating state interests' in order to ensure that the choice of Kansas law is not arbitrary or unfair."

## H.  STATUTORY COMPLIANCE

The general rule is that compliance with applicable state or federal statutes or regulations is some evidence that the defendant exercised due care, Rumsey v. Freeway Manor Minimax (1968), and that the product was not defective or unreasonably dangerous, Rucker v. Norfolk & W. Ry. Co. (1979). Such compliance is generally not considered conclusive, because governmental standards may merely provide minimal requirements, Jonescue v. Jewel Home Shop. Serv. (1973).

Several states provide by statute that compliance with applicable governmental statutes or regulations creates a presumption that a product is not defective or unreasonably dangerous, or a presumption that the defendant exercised due care. See Grundberg v. Upjohn Co. (1991) (Halcion, FDA compliance). Such a provision probably requires the plaintiff to introduce evidence that the statutory or administrative standard is inadequate in some way, or else a verdict on the issue should be directed for the defendant.

The United States Supreme Court in Cipollone v. Liggett Group, Inc. (1992) found express preemption of state common law warning claims under the federal cigarette labeling and advertising act. The Court found no preemption, however, of claims based on fraudulent misrepresentation, concealment, conspiracy, breach of express warranty, or failure to test or research adequately where such testing and research are unrelated to a claim based on cigarette labeling or advertising. The defendant conceded that claims for production and design defects would not be preempted by the act.

The cases divide sharply on the issue of implied statutory preemption in such areas for example as airbags (NTMVSA), pesticide warnings (FIFRA), drug warnings (FDA), and the like. See, e.g., Perry v. Mercedes Benz of North America, Inc. (1992) (airbag); Papas v. Upjohn Co. (1991) (pesticide); *Grundberg* supra (drug). Where such preemption is found, it is usually based on the rationale that the statute is intended to occupy the field of safety regulation, or that a common law remedy would conflict with the goals of the statutory regulation.

The *Cipollone* case may give impetus to such findings of implied preemption, but it should not do so. *Cipollone* was a case of express, not implied, preemption and the Court was badly fractured in its opinion. There is a strong presumption against a finding of implied preemption. See Silkwood v. Kerr–McGee Corp. (1984). This is because a statutory standard is usually the result of political compromise. It is not intended to be as demanding as a common law standard, or to replace common law remedies where no alternative statutory remedy is provided. A legislature can either expressly preempt, or expressly provide against preemption. See Palmer v. Liggett Group, Inc. (1986). Absent such an express statement one way or the other, the courts should be very reluctant to find implied statutory preemption.

## I.  CONTRACT SPECIFICATIONS DEFENSE

### 1.  NONGOVERNMENT SPECIFICATIONS

There is some authority for the proposition that one who manufactures a product in accordance with the specifications of a nongovernment purchaser is not strictly liable for a defect in design unless the danger is obvious. Lesnefsky v. Fischer & Porter Co., Inc. (1981). Nor was the manufacturer liable in negligence, said the *Lesnefsky* court, since there was no basis for finding that the defendant knew of the defect and it had no duty to undertake an independent safety investigation.

The court in Johnston v. United States (1983) said the contract specifications defense for nongovernment specifications protects the contractor from liability only for ordinary negligence, but not where the specifications "are so defective and dangerous that a reasonably competent contractor 'would realize that there was a grave chance that his product would be dangerously unsafe'." The defense, said the court in *Johnston,* "does not apply to actions grounded in strict liability." Similarly, the court in Michalko v. Cooke Color and Chem. Corp. (1982) held that a contractor who rebuilt a transfer press according to the specifications of the owner could be held strictly liable for injuries caused by the lack of safety devices on the machine.

## 2.  GOVERNMENT SPECIFICATIONS

The United States Supreme Court established a federal government contract defense as a matter of federal common law by a 5–4 vote in Boyle v. United Technologies Corp. (1988).  Under this defense a contractor is immune from liability for injuries caused by a defectively designed product supplied to the government in accordance with government contract specifications.  The court set forth four elements necessary to establish the defense:  (1) the approval of the design by the United States must involve a "discretionary function", as that term is used in the Federal Tort Claims Act, 28 U.S.C. § 1346(b);  (2) the United States must have "approved reasonably precise specifications";  (3) the product must have "conformed to those specifications";  and (4) the supplier must have "warned the United States about the dangers in the use of the equipment that were known to the supplier but not to the United States."

Cases prior to *Boyle* had limited the scope of the federal government contract defense to military procurement contracts.  Decisions since *Boyle* divide on the issue of whether the defense applies only to military procurement, or to all government contracts.  Compare Nielsen v. George Diamond Vogel Paint Co. (1990) (military procurement only) with Garner v. Santoro (1989) (all government contracts).  The language and rationale of *Boyle* are broad enough to extend the defense to all government contracts.

*Boyle* involved an alleged design defect. The court in Mitchell v. Lone Star Ammunition, Inc. (1990) said the defense did not apply to a manufacturing defect, since a defect in manufacture indicated that the product did not comply with the design specifications of the contract. The court here disregarded the fact that design standards controlling production may determine the nature and frequency of manufacturing defects.

Even though the contractor may have no duty to warn the government, because the government is aware of the dangers associated with a product, several courts have held that the contractor may nevertheless owe a duty to warn third persons of those dangers. See, e.g., Dorse v. Eagle–Picher Industries, Inc. (1990). The correctness of such decisions depends on whether the duty to warn described in the fourth element of the *Boyle* formulation is intended to be exclusive.

There are apparently no cases indicating whether a government contractor can be liable for misrepresentation. Presumably it can be, either to the government or to third parties, since a misrepresentation would undercut the contractor's otherwise satisfactory performance of its contract.

*Boyle* indicated that a contractor would be liable if the product lacked a safety feature not dealt with in the specifications, or if the government merely ordered a "stock" product by "model number." The court in Trevino v. General Dynamics Corp. (1989) took this reasoning a step further, holding that mere "rubber stamp" approval of contract specifications by the government would not relieve a contractor of liability for design defects. The court said, however, that if there were substantial review by the government, the contractor immunity could not be circumvented by a showing that "the government official doing the review was incompetent or negligent."

There may be a state government contractor defense. In Montgomery v. City of Chicago (1991) the court said a state contractor had no duty to determine the adequacy of design specifications unless they were so dangerous that no reasonable contractor would follow them. The state contractor may have less protection than the federal contractor, since the cases indicate that the federal contractor is relieved from liability as long as the danger is known to the government. Stout v. Borg–Warner Corp. (1991). Such knowledge on the part of the government would not protect the state contractor under *Montgomery*, however, where the design specifications were so dangerous that no reasonable contractor would follow them.

## J.  STATUTES OF LIMITATIONS
### 1.  THE APPLICABLE STATUTE

In a products case there may be two or more statutes of limitations that can apply to a cause of action. One approach is to allow the plaintiff to rely on a warranty statute for a warranty claim, and a tort or personal injury statute for tort claims, as in Garcia v. Texas Instruments, Inc. (1980). Another is to look to the gist of the action, and apply only the tort or personal injury statute even to a claim based on breach of warranty. This was the approach taken in Taylor v. Ford Motor Co. (1991), where the court applied the tort statute of limitations to a warranty claim for personal injuries since, said the court, personal injury damages have been traditionally associated with tort law.

Another area of potential overlap concerns statutes of repose for improvements to realty. A "statute of repose" is a term used to describe a statute of limitations whose period begins to run from a fixed date regardless of when the claimant is injured or has reason to know of the injury. In the case of realty improvement statutes, the period typically begins to run from completion of the improvement, for a period of between four to twelve years. Here the issue usually is whether or not the realty statute of limitations preempts other limitations statutes.

The question of whether a realty statute of repose applies to the supply of a product generally turns on the court's interpretation of whether or not the product must be specially or particularly supplied for the improvement involved. Thus in Witham v. Whiting Corp. (1992) the court held that a 40–ton crane made to order for a steel plant was an improvement to which the state's 10–year statute of repose applied. Similarly, the court in Swanson Furniture Co. of Marshfield, Inc. v. Advance Transformer Co. (1982) said that in order for the statute to apply the product must be "deliberately directed towards or chosen for a particular project for real property improvement." By contrast, the court in Catanzaro v. Wasco Products, Inc. (1985) held that a manufacturer of a skylight-skydome not made to specifications was nevertheless covered by the realty statute. In Luzadder v. Despatch Oven Co. (1986), the court held the statute did not apply to product manufacturers whose products merely happened to be incorporated into a realty improvement.

A number of states have enacted general statutes of repose, intended to apply to all products liability actions regardless of whether any other statute of limitations otherwise applies. Usually these statutes begin to run from the date of first sale for use or consumption, e.g., Tenn. Code Ann. § 29–28–103 (10–year period).

These general statutes of repose have not always been given comprehensive application to products liability suits, however. The federal court of appeals in Guy v. E.I. DuPont de Nemours & Co. (1986) held that North Carolina's statute did not apply to cumulative injuries, which were not personal injury claims within the intent of the statute. The Georgia Supreme Court, on certification from the federal court of appeals for the Eleventh Circuit, held in Hatcher v. Allied Prod. Corp. (1986)

that Georgia's statute applied only to strict liability claims against manufacturers.

## 2. DATE OF ACCRUAL

The accrual date (the time at which the period of the statute of limitations begins to run) may vary depending on the statutory language or the applicable rule adopted by the court. Repose statutes usually expressly provide when the period begins to run. Thus the warranty statute of limitations, UCC § 2–725, begins to run from the time when tender of delivery of the goods is made. As noted in the previous section, realty improvement statutes run from the date of completion of the improvement; and general products liability repose statutes run from the date of first sale for use or consumption. The length of the statutory period varies from statute to statute.

The warranty statute of limitations provides that when a warranty "explicitly extends to future performance of the goods and discovery of the breach must await the time of such performance the cause of action accrues when the breach is or should have been discovered." UCC § 2–725(2). This future-performance rule applies if the seller guarantees performance for a specified time. R.W. Murray Co. v. Shatterproof Glass Corp. (1983) (curtain wall guaranteed free of defects in material or workmanship for 10 years, and free of moisture accumulation and dust collection for 20 years). In

Balog v. Center Art Gallery–Hawaii, Inc. (1990) the court said the certification of an art work as authentic was an explicit warranty of future performance causing the warranty limitations period to run from the date of reasonable discovery of the breach, rather than the date of sale. Stumler v. Ferry–Morse Seed Co. (1981) said most courts hold that an implied warranty cannot explicitly extend to future performance.

The court in Rollins v. Cherokee Warehouses, Inc. (1986), held that the Tennessee general statute of repose for products liability begins to run from the date of sale of a substantially rebuilt and resold machine. But in Kochins v. Linden–Alimak, Inc. (1986), the court held that this statute did not begin to run from the time of delivery of an instruction manual after the product was sold, because the manual was not a "product," or alternatively because it was not a "new" product but simply a replacement of the original manual.

Statutes of limitations other than statutes of repose generally begin to run at one of three times: 1) date of injury, Much v. Sturm, Ruger & Co., Inc. (1980); 2) date when the plaintiff had reason to know of the claim, Sahlie v. Johns–Manville Sales Corp. (1983); or 3) date when the plaintiff in the exercise of reasonable care should have known of the claim, Ohler v. Tacoma General Hosp. (1979). The last accrual date (reasonable discovery) is the most favorable to the plaintiff, and it is probably the one most widely used. Discovery under this rule has been held to mean that the plaintiff "in the exercise of reasonable diligence should have discovered not only that he has been injured but also that his injury may have been caused by the defendant's conduct." Raymond v. Eli Lilly & Co. (1977). The *Ohler* court, supra, made this rule clearer by saying that the action does not accrue until the plaintiff "reasonably should have discovered all the essential elements of her possible cause of action."

By amendment, § 309(a)(1) (1986), Congress changed 42 U.S.C. § 9601 et seq. (CERCLA) so as to preempt state statute of limitations accrual rules for personal injury or property damage caused by the release from a facility of a hazardous substance, pollutant or contaminant into the environment. The amendment fixes a uniform accrual date for such state statutes running from the time when the plaintiff knew or had reason to know of her or his injury. The court in Covalt v. Carey Canada, Inc. (1988) held that this tolling provision did not apply to workplace exposure to asbestos, since the contaminant was not "released into the environment from a facility" within the meaning of the statute.

Sometimes a plaintiff will suffer a discoverable injury, and then later the injury will develop into a different injury or disease. In Potts v. Celotex Corp. (1990) the court said the statute of limitations for plaintiff's mesothelioma began to run against the defendant asbestos manufacturer when that disease was diagnosed, not when the plaintiff learned earlier that he had contracted asbestosis from the product. The court said a great majority of courts follow this rule, and that it would be "unfair to allow the manifestation of one disease caused by exposure to asbestos to preclude recovery for a second, unrelated disease" caused by that exposure.

The right of contribution is usually governed by statute, with the period running from date of judgment or payment, see, e.g., Unif. Contrib. Among Tortfeasors Act § 3 (1955). The period for bringing an indemnity action has variously been held to run from date of sale from the indemnitor to the indemnitee, Caruloff v. Emerson Radio & Phonograph Corp. (1971), the date of discovery of the injury, Alabama Great So. R. Co. v. Allied Chem. Corp. (1972), or the date of payment of the underlying claim, Davidson Lumber Sales, Inc. v. Bonneville Investment, Inc. (1990).

## 3. TOLLING EXCEPTIONS

The jurisdictions, by express statutory exception or by judicial construction, have imposed tolling exceptions on the various statutory dates of accrual. The statutory period can be tolled, or stayed, by the occurrence of an event that keeps the period from beginning or from continuing to run as it would otherwise do in the absence of the event's occurrence. Plaintiff's minority typically tolls the statute, as does fraudulent concealment, continuing duty to warn, and absence of the defendant from the jurisdiction. Under New Jersey law, a statute of limitations did not run against a school board acting in its governmental capacity, in a claim against an asbestos manufacturer for asbestos removal costs. Livingston Bd. of Educ. v. U.S. Gypsum Co. (1991).

Some courts are unwilling to engraft tolling exceptions onto statutes of repose by judicial construction, since the exceptions tend to defeat the underlying policy of the repose statute itself. Thus the court in Tolen v. A.H. Robins Co., Inc. (1983) refused to toll the statute of repose for fraudulent concealment. Wilson v. Dake Corp. (1980) refused to toll the repose statute based on a continuing duty to warn. Erickson Air–Crane Co. v. United Technologies Corp. (1986) held the statute of repose was not tolled by post-sale misrepresentations as to the useful life of the product. Such decisions are often thought to be controlled by the exclusive language of the statute, but they need not be. Where the defendant's conduct estops him from relying on the statute, the statute's provisions simply do not apply.

## 4.  CONSTITUTIONAL QUESTIONS

Miscellaneous questions arise regarding the constitutionality of statutes of limitations. The United States Supreme Court in G. D. Searle & Co. v. Cohn (1982) held that a New Jersey rule tolling the statute against out-of-state corporations having no in-state agent for service of process was constitutional under the due process and equal protection clauses, even though the corporation was subject to service of process by long-arm jurisdiction. The case was remanded where it was determined that the New Jersey rule violated the commerce clause. Anson v. American Motors Corp. (1987) held that the provision of a discovery rule for personal injury but not for wrongful death claims was an unconstitutional limitation of damages and a denial of equal protection in wrongful death cases. In Davis v. Dow Chem. Corp. (1987), the court held that the Arizona wrongful death statute, providing for the accrual of the cause of action at the date of death, would be unconstitutional under the state constitution if not construed to allow for reasonable discovery of the cause of action. Barrio v. San Manuel Div. Hosp. for Magma Copper Co. (1984) held that a statute requiring a child under the age of seven to bring its medical malpractice action by age ten, or else be barred, was unconstitutional.

By far the largest number of cases in this area concern the constitutionality of general statutes of repose for products liability. These statutes have been attacked on various state and federal constitutional grounds, including equal protection, due process, privileges and immunities, and "open court" provisions. As the court in Hanson v. Williams County (1986) noted, in holding the North

Dakota statute of repose unconstitutional, "many courts have found [such statutes] to be unconstitutional" because of the "harsh result" that "bars a cause of action before the injury occurs." The court in Daily v. New Britain Machine Co. (1986), in upholding the Connecticut statute, concluded that a "majority of jurisdictions [have] upheld the constitutionality of similar statutes of repose against attacks on equal protection grounds." It is not clear, however, whether a majority of courts have upheld such statutes against all grounds of constitutional attack, and the tide seems to be running against their constitutionality.

Similar constitutional attacks have been made against statutes of repose for realty improvements, with the cases again going both ways. See Perkins v. Northeastern Log Homes (1991), and Chp. 198B Bldg Code (Ky Laws 1992). Curiously, there appear to be no cases attacking the constitutionality of warranty statutes of repose. Perhaps this is because the warranty statute is frequently found not to be exclusive where personal injury or property damage is involved, so that the plaintiff can bring his claim under another statute of limitations. Also, it is in the case of personal injuries involving innocent consumers that the harshness of the absolute cutoff of a cause of action before it ever arises seems most pronounced, so that the problem may be less acute in warranty cases involving economic loss.

## K.  STATUTORY RETRENCHMENTS

A number of state legislatures have enacted statutes cutting back on consumer rights in the area of products liability, in an attempt to meet a perceived crisis in the availability and affordability of liability insurance owing to a claimed mushrooming of the quantity of litigation and the size of verdicts.  The accuracy of such perceptions and claims is the subject of much dispute.  In some instances the statutes are directed toward tort law in general including products liability, and in others toward specific fields of tort litigation such as products liability.  A number of attempts have been made to pass similar statutes on a federal level, but so far without success.

The statutes vary greatly from state to state, both with regard to the subjects covered and the type of change made.  The issues cover a wide spectrum of subjects, including:  limitations on the amount of chargeable contingent fees;  elimination of the collateral source rule;  provision for periodic payment of judgments;  elimination of strict liability, and the adoption of a product state-of-the-art defense;  elimination or restriction of recovery for punitive damages;  the elimination or restriction of joint liability for co-tortfeasors;  adoption of statutes of repose;  and placing a limit on the recoverable amount of damages for pain and suffering, mental distress, and the like.

As noted in the previous section, a number of attacks have been made on the constitutionality of statutes of repose.  The Supreme Court of Florida in Smith v. Department of Ins. (1987) declared that state's $450,000 tort cap on recoverable noneconomic losses to be unconstitutional under a state constitutional provision providing a right of access to the courts.  The limitation would be constitutional, the court said, if an alternative remedy were provided, or a showing of overpowering public necessity for the limitation were made.  No alternative remedy was provided, nor was such a showing of public necessity made here.  In Brannigan v. Usitalo (1991) the court held that a state statute limiting recoverable noneconomic damages to $875,000 violated equal protection rights guaranteed by the state constitution.

It remains to be seen whether such statutory retrenchments will generally be upheld as constitutional, and if so whether they will significantly reduce insurance rates or the amount of litigation and damages recovered.  Judging from the effect of prior retrenching enactments in the areas of medical malpractice and products liability, it seems unlikely that these changes will have any significant impact on liability insurance rates—which are more likely controlled by market considerations than by tort law.  Assuming the amount of tort litigation and verdicts is increasing, it does not follow that the increase is either good or bad. Such an increase, moreover, is not particularly indicative of the status of tort claims, since the vast majority of tort claims made are never litigated.

# CHAPTER V

# PRODUCTION AND DESIGN DEFECTS

## A. PRODUCTION DEFECTS

Courts often refer to a manufacturing or production flaw as distinct from a design defect. "In manufacturing defect cases, the plaintiff proves that the product is defective by simply showing that it does not conform to the manufacturer's specifications." Singleton v. International Harvester Co. (1981). This definition does not imply that the manufacturer failed to exercise due care, since liability can be imposed even when the evidence shows there is no practical way of discovering or preventing the defect. Vlases v. Montgomery Ward & Co. (1967) (avian leukosis in baby chickens, scientifically undetectable).

Moreover, the rule appears to indicate that the manufacturer can set its own standard. If, for example, a manufacturer determined that a 20% failure rate was acceptable, none of the products falling within this range of failure should be considered defective. Cf. Agoos Kid Co. v. Blumenthal Import Corp. (1932) ("Bagdad goat skins dry salted.... In the trade it is considered that a lot is normal if it does not appear that more than one and one half percent, or at most three percent, are improperly cured and therefore worthless."). Such a result should not be inferred from the rule, however. The better approach is to compare an aberrant product with otherwise similar units of the manufacturer to determine if it departs materially from the design specifications, formula or performance of the other units. If there is such a departure, it should be no defense that the departure was either intended or expected.

Probably what is contemplated by the concept of production defect is random defectiveness. A bottle of "Squirt" containing a decomposed mouse, as in Shoshone Coca–Cola Bott. Co. v. Dolinski (1966), is unusual and clearly recognizable as aberrant. Not all production defect cases fall into that category, however. For example, the defective weld in the helicopter tail in Krause v. Sud–Aviation (1969) may or may not have been a production defect. One expert testified that the weld "definitely [lacked] root penetration", while two other experts testified that their examination "revealed nothing unusual about the weld." Where expert testimony is necessary to establish defectiveness, the defect cannot be considered an aberration in the sense of a deviation from the general understanding. Consumer expectations can however determine defectiveness once expert testimony is offered as the basis for such expectations.

The idea of randomness is not always a useful means of distinguishing production from design defects, if the idea is intended to refer to the rate of failure. The failure rate of a product can turn on the environment of use, as well as on the formula for construction. A metal, for example, might not withstand certain foreseeable uses, see Cronin v. J.B.E. Olson Corp. (1972), although it may be suitable for most other uses. Foreseeability of use is relevant in both production and design defect cases.

"The majority of courts," said the court in Reed v. Tiffin Motor Homes, Inc. (1982), "have found in design defect cases, as opposed to manufacturing defect cases, that state of the art and industry standards are relevant to show both the reasonableness of the design ... and that the product was dangerous beyond the expectations of the ordinary consumer." Some states, however, by statute admit evidence of state of the art and industry custom on the issue of defectiveness in both design and production defect cases, e.g., Tenn. Code Ann. § 29–28–105. Also, as discussed in Chapter I on the issue of defectiveness, some courts apply an "unavoidably unsafe" rationale to production defect cases. Under this approach, the scientific practicability of discovering or preventing dangers in a useful product is taken into account in determining whether the product is defective.

The application of strict liability to production defects serves as a catalyst for applying such liability to design cases. Alternatively, use of the standards of state of the art and industry custom in design cases may impose pressure for the adoption of like standards in production defect cases.

## B.  DESIGN DEFECTS
### 1.  THE THEORY OF LIABILITY

The court in Prentis v. Yale Mfg. Co. (1984) (alleged defectively designed forklift without a seat or platform for the operator) defined a design defect as follows:

[T]he overwhelming consensus among courts in deciding defective design cases is in the use of some form of risk-utility analysis. . . .

The risk-utility balancing test is merely a detailed version of Judge Learned Hand's negligence calculus. See United States v. Carroll Towing Co. (1947). As Dean Prosser has pointed out, the liability of the manufacturer rests "upon a departure from proper standards of care, so that the tort is essentially a matter of negligence".

Although many courts have insisted that the risk-utility tests they are applying are not negligence tests because their focus is on the *product* rather than the manufacturer's *conduct* . . . the distinction on closer examination appears to be nothing more than semantic. As a common sense matter, the jury weighs competing factors presented in evidence about the judgment or decision (*i.e., conduct* ) of the manufacturer.

*Prentis* focused on the conduct of the manufacturer in determining the standard of liability for defective design. This approach would not result in the same negligence analysis for nonmanufacturing sellers, since they lack the manufacturer's expert knowledge that is necessary to make a risk-benefit evaluation of the product's safety.

Not all courts consider evidence of custom of the industry as relevant in design defect cases based on strict liability. In Grimshaw v. Ford Motor Co. (1981), the California Court of Appeal held that the trial court did not err in refusing to instruct the jury, in connection with the risk-benefit test, that it could consider the extent to which the defendant's "design and manufacture matched the average quality of other automobiles and the extent to which its design and manufacture deviated from the norm for automobiles designed and manufactured at the same point in time." This refusal was proper because "[i]n a strict products liability case, industry custom or usage is irrelevant to the issue of defect." The relevant considerations in applying the risk-benefit standard, the court said, include "the gravity of the danger posed by the challenged design, the likelihood that such dangers would occur, the mechanical feasibility of a safer alternative design, and the adverse consequences to the product and to the consumer that would result from an alternative design."

It is apparent that the risk-benefit test as applied by *Grimshaw* and by many other courts is not the same as a negligence test. A design may in fact be practicable and economical even though a manufacturer reasonably does not know of its availability. In this connection, the reader should review the definitions of defectiveness in Chapter I.

There are some other significant variations on the definition of design defectiveness for strict liability. In Dart v. Wiebe Mfg., Inc. (1985), the court said: "In a negligence case, the inquiry focuses on the reasonableness of the manufacturer's choice of design in light of the knowledge available at the time of manufacture. Under strict liability, however, knowledge of the 'danger in fact' as revealed by the accident and the testimony at trial is imputed to the manufacturer." This strict liability test also sidesteps negligence, since available knowledge and skills at the date of trial may be greater than at the time of manufacture years previously.

The California Supreme Court in Barker v. Lull Engineering Co., Inc. (1978) established a two-prong test for determining design defectiveness in strict liability:

First, a product may be found defective in design if the plaintiff establishes that the product failed to perform as safely as an ordinary consumer would expect when used in an intended or reasonably foreseeable manner. Second, a product may alternatively be found defective in design if the plaintiff demonstrates that the product's design proximately caused his injury and the defendant fails to establish, in light of the relevant factors, that, on balance, the benefits of the challenged design outweigh the risk of danger inherent in such design.

The reason for shifting the burden of proof on the risk-benefit balancing test, the court said, was because this test "introduces an element which 'rings of negligence' ", and the injured plaintiff should "not be burdened with proving such an element in strict liability."

The court in Lavespere v. Niagara Machine & Tool Works (1990) placed the burden of proof on the plaintiff to show how an alternative design would have decreased the risk, how its adoption would have affected the manufacturer's burden of production, and how the product's utility would have been affected by the alternative design. But in Karns v. Emerson Elec. Co. (1987) the court held the plaintiff was not required to show a safer design if the design posed a danger that exceeded the expectations of the ordinary consumer.

As the court said in O'Brien v. Muskin Corp. (1983)—a case involving an allegedly unreasonably slippery vinyl swimming pool—a product may be so dangerous or so lacking in social utility that a jury can find it should not have been marketed at all.

The evaluation of the utility of a product also involves the relative need for that product; some products are essentials, while others are luxuries. A product that fills a critical need and can be designed in only one way should be viewed differently from a luxury item. Still other products, including some for which no alternative exists, are so dangerous and of such little use that under the risk-utility analysis, a manufacturer would bear the cost of liability of harm to others. That cost might dissuade a manufacturer from placing the product on the market, even if the product has been made as safely as possible.

Similarly, in Gilboy v. American Tobacco Co. (1991) the court held that cigarettes may be found unreasonably dangerous per se, i.e., so dangerous that they should not have been marketed at all. A Louisiana statute repealing the common law rule of unreasonable danger per se was not retroactive and therefore did not apply to this case.

## 2. POLYCENTRICITY

Some courts and commentators have expressed concern about the propriety of submitting complex design issues to a jury that lacks the kind of expert knowledge thought necessary to judge such issues. The court expressed this concern in Dawson v. Chrysler Corp. (1980), where the plaintiff alleged that his automobile lacked sufficient bodily integrity to withstand a side impact at a relatively low speed. Defendant contended that "deformation of the body of the vehicle is desirable in most crashes because it absorbs the impact of the crash and decreases the rate of deceleration on the occupants of the vehicle."

The court reluctantly affirmed a $2 million jury verdict for the plaintiff, noting that "while the jury found Chrysler liable for not producing a rigid enough vehicular frame, a factfinder in another case might well hold the manufacturer liable for producing a frame that is too rigid." It further noted that jury verdicts in product design cases might well conflict with broad "national economic and social concerns", such as the design of "smaller, more fuel-efficient cars." The court felt it had no alternative but to sustain the verdict in this case, however, absent controlling legislation, since the plaintiff made out a submissible jury question on which there was a conflict of evidence.

Sometimes conscious design decisions are described as "polycentric" or "many-centered problems, in which each point for decision is related to all the others as are the strands of a spider web. If one strand is pulled, a complex pattern of readjustment will occur throughout the entire web." Bowman v. General Motors Corp. (1977). Inadvertent design flaws, said the court in *Bowman*, are like manufacturing flaws in that both are "subject to measurement against a built-in *objective* standard or norm of proper manufacture or design." But where a conscious design choice has caused an injury,

we are faced with quite a different problem; for there is no built-in objective standard by which the jury can measure the alleged defect. This result stems, at least in part, from the fact that a conscious design choice necessarily involves a trade-off among safety, utility, and cost. The trade-off may be obvious and may also be acceptable to the consumer. At the very least, it reflects the manufacturer's judgment of what would be acceptable if the terms of the trade-off were publicly known. However, the process of evaluating the trade-off, which represents the manufacturer's distillation of the forces of the marketplace, is a sophisticated one which complicates the process of products liability adjudication.

The *Bowman* court nevertheless felt that by using the "unreasonably dangerous" concept, formulated in terms of "a risk-utility balancing test", a jury could properly evaluate conscious design decisions. They should be instructed to consider the likelihood and seriousness of potential injury, the ability of the manufacturer to eliminate any unsafe characteristic without impairing the usefulness or significantly increasing the cost of the product, and the extent to which the danger would be beyond that expected by the ordinary consumer taking into account the ability of the manufacturer to give a meaningful warning.

Any distinction between conscious and inadvertent design decisions for purposes of determining the suitability of design cases for litigation is questionable. Presumably in the vast majority of design decisions the manufacturer does not fully anticipate or appreciate the likelihood of serious injury from the foreseeable use of its product as designed, for if it did then the marketing of the product with such foreknowledge could well give rise to a claim of punitive damages for manufacturing recklessness or conscious indifference to the safety of the public.

The argument that design decisions are too complex to be evaluated by a jury cuts too far, since the problem of issue complexity extends to many areas of the law. Whenever expert testimony is required to make out a submissible case, the issue by its nature is complex.

Opponents of the polycentricity argument contend that proper design judgments are not polycentric. A primary design consideration should be one of determining the level of design safety that is consonant with reasonable cost and utility. It is only when the manufacturer places market considerations above those of safety in designing a product that a design is likely to be judged unreasonably dangerous.

### 3. THE RELATION OF DESIGN AND WARNING DEFECTS

There is not always a bright line between design and warning defects. While one tends to think of a design as the product of a mechanical or engineering decision, and a warning as the result of a written or oral communication, this distinction does not always hold true. In Hollinger v. Wagner Min. Equip. Co. (1981), the plaintiff was held to have alleged a design defect based on the absence of an "automatic warning device" on a scooptram. Similarly, in Simms v. Thiede (1990) the lack of a mirror on an excavator was held to be a design defect, creating a blind spot that led to the plaintiff bystander's injury. The design defects in both of these cases involved the lack of a mechanically engineered warning.

Conversely, the placement of written warning labels and notices, and their content and form, may involve engineering design decisions or close collaboration with engineers. Warning and design decisions also share the feature of being generic to a whole line of products. Therefore, questions of the relevancy of industry custom and state of the art may be common to both types of defect.

In some cases the courts have held that a manufacturer cannot discharge his duty to design a safer product by an oral or written warning of the danger. This is because in some instances "a user may not have a real alternative to using a dangerous product, as where a worker must either work on a dangerous machine or leave his job." Furthermore, "a warning is not effective in eliminating injuries due to instinctual reactions, momentary inadvertence, or forgetfulness on the part of a worker. One of the primary purposes of safety devices is to guard against such foreseeable situations." So, concluded the court in Uloth v. City Tank Corp. (1978):

> Balanced against the somewhat limited effectiveness of warnings is the designer's ability to

anticipate and protect against possible injuries. If a slight change in design would prevent serious, perhaps fatal, injury, the designer may not avoid liability by simply warning of the possible injury. We think that in such a case the burden to prevent needless injury is best placed on the designer or manufacturer rather than on the individual user of a product.

The rationale for the *Uloth* rule is closely related to the modern proposition that an obvious danger will not necessarily discharge a manufacturer's duty to design a safe product, since a warning merely serves the purpose of making the danger obvious. Relying on this reasoning, the court in Sturm, Ruger & Co. v. Day (1979) held that a warning that a "light accidental blow" on the hammer of defendant's gun "can readily cause the gun to discharge" did not eliminate defendant's duty to design an effective safety mechanism for the gun. The warning would not protect "the 'inadvertent plaintiff' who accidentally dropped the gun", as the plaintiff did here.

In reaching its result, the court in *Day* said:

A number of courts have held that the manufacturer's liability is not precluded merely because the danger from his product is obvious.... We believe that this reasoning applies equally to products whose printed warnings alert the public to hidden dangers as to products whose dangers are patently obvious.

Compliance with a warning may be impractical, necessitating redesign. This was the case in Wheeler v. John Deere Co. (1991). There a warning was disregarded because of the need to remove a protective shield in order to clean a combine auger.

In the typical design case the plaintiff will plead defective design as well as inadequate warning. The warning claim should not be successful if the warning would have made no difference owing to the inadvertent or involuntary conduct of the plaintiff. On the other hand, the claim should not be barred if plaintiff's inadvertence is induced by the lack of a warning, or by a warning which is inadequately communicated as in Rhodes v. Interstate Battery System of America, Inc. (1984). The warning claim should be upheld whenever the plaintiff convinces the fact finder that a warning would have enabled him to avoid the injury. It is possible, of course, that a jury will be more prone to find the presence or absence of a causal effect of a warning on behalf of one party rather than another in a given case, and relative causation may be compared in a comparative fault jurisdiction.

The plaintiff cannot fairly be put to the election of choosing between a theory of design or of warning defect to meet the causation problems just discussed, since he can never be certain which is the better theory on which to proceed or whether he will be successful on one rather than the other.

Also, since warning and design theories sometimes overlap, any such election requirement would prove artificial in overlapping cases.

There are some cases, as will be seen in the warning chapter, in which plaintiff's only theory will be one of failure to warn. Such situations arise where for example the product is made as safely as possible, but contains a latent danger about which the user should be warned. Also, in allergy cases, or cases involving a post-sale duty to warn, the only duty owed may be a warning duty.

## 4.   OBVIOUSNESS OF DANGER

The rule that an obviously dangerous product is as a matter of law not unreasonably dangerous was once widely followed. The principal authority for this rule was Campo v. Scofield (1950), where the plaintiff alleged that an onion-topping machine was unreasonably dangerous because it lacked adequate guards. The court treated the case as if an obviously dangerous product was nondefective:

> We have not yet reached the state where a manufacturer is under the duty of making a machine accident proof or foolproof.... To illustrate, the manufacturer who makes, properly and free of defects, an axe or a buzz saw or an airplane with an exposed propeller, is not liable if one using the axe or buzz saw is cut by it, or if some one working around the airplane comes in contact with the propeller.... In other words,

the manufacturer is under no duty to render a machine or other article "more" safe—as long as the danger to be avoided is obvious and patent to all.

The case is still followed in a number of jurisdictions.

It is not always easy to identify an obvious danger. For example, the court in Bolm v. Triumph Corp. (1973) held that a jury question was presented as to whether the danger created by a metal luggage rack fixed to the top of plaintiff's motorcycle gas tank was obvious. In Lamon v. McDonnell Douglas Corp. (1979), the court held that whether the danger from an unguarded open emergency hatch in an airplane was obvious presented a jury question. Whether a swimming pool created a dangerous illusion of depth was held to be a fact question in Silverman v. Zebersky (1991).

Many courts recognize that the plaintiff who suffers a workplace injury should not be denied recovery on grounds of obviousness of the danger, since the plaintiff's exposure to the danger is not voluntary. Rhoads v. Service Mach. Co. (1971). The rescuer who exposes himself to an obvious danger is not barred from recovery, Guarino v. Mine Safety Appliance Co. (1969).

Moreover, the obvious danger defense conflicts with the defense of assumption of the risk. To establish assumption of the risk "it must be shown that the plaintiff (1) discovered the defect, (2) fully understood the danger it presented, and (3) disregarded this known danger and voluntarily exposed himself or herself to it.... The burden of establishing those requirements is on the defendant, whereas under the patent danger rule the defendant would not be required to prove that the plaintiff was aware of the danger presented and voluntarily exposed himself or herself to it." Gann v. International Harvester Co. of Canada, Ltd. (1986).

Because of the difficulties of defining the obvious or patent danger, the exceptions that have developed to the rule, and the rule's unfairness, a number of modern courts have rejected the rule as a legal bar to recovery in a products liability suit. New York rejected its own *Campo* rule in Micallef v. Miehle Co. (1976), holding that "the openness and obviousness of the danger should be available to the defendant on the issue of whether plaintiff exercised that degree of reasonable care as was required under the circumstances." As the court said in Auburn Mach. Works Co., Inc. v. Jones (1979), in rejecting obviousness as a bar to recovery: "The patent danger doctrine encourages manufacturers to be outrageous in their design, to eliminate safety devices, and to make dangers obvious". See also Holm v. Sponco Mfg., Inc. (1982) (defense rejected—cases reviewed).

The patent danger rule should be distinguished from the defense of common knowledge. For example, in Garrison v. Heublein, Inc. (1982), the court held that the dangers of drinking alcohol are common knowledge, so that alcohol is not an unreasonably dangerous product. It is "common knowledge" that pork must be cooked before being eaten, in order to destroy any trichinae in the raw pork, see Cheli v. Cudahy Bros. Co. (1934). Cases such as these may better be explained by saying that the court finds the product nondefective for policy reasons, and imputes knowledge of the danger to the public as a means of reaching this result.

While there may be a duty to eliminate obvious dangers by redesign of a product, it is unlikely that a court will find a duty to warn of the truly obvious danger. The Tenn. Prod. Liab. Act, Tenn. Code Ann. § 29–28–105(d), states that a product "is not unreasonably dangerous because of failure to adequately warn of a danger or hazard that is apparent to the ordinary user." In the case of an obvious danger, a warning is redundant.

## 5.  CRASHWORTHINESS

Crashworthiness is a term used to describe the capability of a product to protect against increased injury from an accident caused by something or someone other than the product. The cases frequently arise in connection with automobile collisions, as for example with regard to fuel tank crashworthiness, General Motors Corp. v. Edwards (1985), rooftop rollover capability, Shipp v. General Motors Corp. (1985), and the like. They may arise in a variety of other contexts, however, such as where a fire extinguisher fails to work, a burglar alarm malfunctions, a grain harvester lacks an emergency shutoff device, and so forth.

The early approach was to hold that there was no duty to design a product to protect against an accident caused by a source other than the product. Evans v. General Motors Corp. (1966). This approach has been widely rejected, and most courts find a duty to reasonably design against foreseeable accidents. Huff v. White Motor Corp. (1977).

Most of the crashworthiness cases today center around the question of whether the damages must be apportioned between the nonproduct and the product causes of the injury; and if apportionment is required, who has the burden of proof on the issue. Some cases place the burden of apportionment on the plaintiff, as in Harvey v. General Motors Corp. (1989), and others place it on the defendant, Blankenship v. General Motors Corp. (1991). Still others, as in General Motors Corp. v. Edwards (1985), treat the product manufacturer as a joint tortfeasor and hold it jointly and severally liable with any other cause of the accident.

The usual common law rule is to hold cotortfeasors jointly and severally liable where the damages are as a practical matter indivisible. There is no reason for applying a different rule in the so-called crashworthiness cases.

The fact that a court recognizes a manufacturing duty to design a product so as to protect against foreseeable accidents does not mean that the manufacturer will be liable for increased product-related injuries from all accidents. The accident must be foreseeable. Thus, in Daniell v. Ford Motor Co. (1984), for example, the court held it was unforeseeable that the plaintiff would lock herself in the trunk of her car in an attempt to commit suicide. She could not recover for the unforeseeable injuries resulting from the lack of an internal release of the locking mechanism, when she later changed her mind and tried to get out of the trunk.

# CHAPTER VI

# INADEQUATE WARNINGS AND INSTRUCTIONS, AND MISREPRESENTATIONS

## A. WARNINGS AND INSTRUCTIONS

### 1. IN GENERAL

As noted in the previous chapter, the plaintiff will typically allege a failure to warn, along with a design defect count, in a products liability suit. The rule stated in Gosewisch v. American Honda Motor Co. (1987) is widely followed:

A plaintiff is not required to make an election between pursuing a case on a strict products liability theory of either design defect or failure to warn. A plaintiff may proceed with both theories if both are viable. Plaintiffs are allowed to plead theories in the alternative ... and the same set of facts may present more than one theory of recovery. See, e.g., Schneider v. Cessna Aircraft Co., 150 Ariz. 153, 722 P.2d 321 (App. 1985) (plaintiffs proceeded simultaneously with theories of defective design, improper instructions, and failure to warn); Brown v. Sears, Roebuck & Co., 136 Ariz. 556, 667 P.2d 750 (App. 1983) (genuine issue of material fact concerning both alleged design defect and failure to warn).

210

A warning is distinguished from an instruction in that instructions are calculated primarily to secure the efficient use of a product, while warnings are designed to insure safe use. The distinction is well illustrated by Panther Oil & Grease Mfg. Co. v. Segerstrom (1955). Plaintiff suffered a fire loss from the explosion of a can of roof primer that was being heated by some unskilled workmen. The instruction pamphlet stated: "Do Not Heat or Thin.... When either is done, the waterproofing qualities ... are damaged." In rejecting defendants' contention that plaintiff was guilty of contributory negligence by failing to heed these instructions, the court said: "The injunctions both as to heating and thinning are directed toward the mere matter of utility. There is no warning or suggestion that the heating of it would or might pose a hazard of any sort or a consequence other than as stated." The instructions for assembly of a refracting telescope in Midgley v. S.S. Kresge Co. (1976)—though presumably accurate in every respect—were nevertheless inadequate as a warning since they failed to warn of the risk of eye damage from misassembly.

To be adequate, a warning must describe the nature and the extent of the danger involved. A general statement on the package insert of a mammary prosthesis warning regarding the danger of deflation could be found inadequate, said the court in Perfetti v. McGhan Medical (1983). Although the surgeon who performed the prosthesis implant "knew generally of the danger of deflation, he had only minimum knowledge of delayed inflation at the time the prosthesis was implanted. The surgeon expected the prosthesis to last from 10 to 15 years and would not have used the prosthesis if he had been aware of the danger resulting from wear due to a fold in the prosthesis."

A jury could find that a warning on a dishwasher soap was inadequate, the court said in Fyssakis v. Knight Equip. Corp. (1992). The warning stated that the soap was corrosive, but it did not warn that the product could cause blindness. Similarly, in Little v. Liquid Air Corp. (1991) the court said a jury could find that the warning accompanying defendant's propane gas was inadequate. The gas was odorized, and the accompanying data sheet stated that the gas was flammable and explosive and that the area should be evacuated in the event of a gas leak or spill. There was no warning, however, of the risk of nasal fatigue which would cause the gas to cease to be detectable by smell after a period of exposure. The plaintiffs waited for what they considered to be an appropriate length of time after a gas leak and its attempted repair—until they could no longer smell the gas— and were then injured by an explosion when one of them lit a cigarette in the work area. The case has been ordered to be reheard en banc.

The warning may need to detail not only the toxic qualities of a product, as in Boyl v. California Chem. Co. (1963), but also a safe means of disposal. There a weed killer, Triox, was conspicuously labeled as a strong poison, and the user was warned to "wash thoroughly and destroy" the container as soon as it was empty.  Plaintiff used a spray tank to apply the weed killer, and rinsed the tank with a garden hose pouring the rinse water onto rough grass in her back yard.  Five days later while sunbathing in the area where she had poured the rinse water, plaintiff was badly burned from the residue of the rinse still on the ground.  The court held that "defendant knew or should have known of the stable quality and long-lasting contamination propensities of the sodium arsenite contained in the Triox solution upon the earth", and could be held to a duty to give "some reasonable notice or warning concerning a safe disposal of the rinse residue".

A manufacturer may be required to warn of the absence of an antidote in the case of a dangerous poison.  In Rumsey v. Freeway Manor Minimax (1968), plaintiff's deceased, a three-year-old, consumed some roach poison containing thallium. The boy was taken to a doctor, who lost valuable time in a vain effort to find a specific antidote to thallium.  A stomach pump was not used until after a fatal amount of the poison had been absorbed into the boy's system.  The court held that a common law duty to warn of the extent of the danger had been breached by the defendant manufacturer in failing to warn of the absence of a specific antidote.

A manufacturer should take account of the environment in which its product will be used when

fashioning warnings. In Campos v. Firestone Tire
& Rubber Co. (1984), for example, the court said
that a tire assembly warning might have to be
presented in pictures and symbols to be effective
for illiterate workers. Similarly, in Hubbard–Hall
Chem. Co. v. Silverman (1965), the court said a jury
could reasonably find that the defendant should
have foreseen its highly toxic insecticide would be
used by illiterate workers, so the warning label
could be found inadequate because it lacked "a
skull and bones or other comparable symbols or
hieroglyphics."

The defendant may be required to anticipate the
foreseeable misuse of its product in warning of
dangers associated with the product's use. In Evridge v. American Honda Motor Co. (1985), the
court said a jury could find the defendants failed to
give sufficient warning of the dangers of doubling
on a motorbike. "In formulating their warning,
the defendants were required to take into account
that the Honda Express was designed and intended
for the use of children". In Germann v. F.L.
Smithe Machine Co. (1986), the court said that
even though the defendant manufacturer's press
was reasonably designed, the manufacturer could
still be held liable for failure to warn of the necessity of replacing a safety bar that had to be removed for expectable and frequent maintenance
and repair. It was foreseeable that the bar would
be left off, as occurred in this case, after such
maintenance and repair.

In many instances a warning is required in order to enable the plaintiff to use the product in such a way as to avoid a concealed danger.  In DCR Inc. v. Peak Alarm Co. (1983), plaintiff successfully contended that had he been warned of the vulnerability of defendant's burglar alarm to burglar deactivation, and of an "inexpensive way to protect its alarm systems against the risk of such deactivation," he could have avoided his burglary loss. Likewise, in Laaperi v. Sears, Roebuck & Co., Inc. (1986), the plaintiff stated a cause of action for defendant's failure to warn that its smoke detector was subject to a fire short-out.  "He contended that had he been warned of this danger, he would have purchased a battery-powered smoke detector as a back-up or taken some other precaution, such as wiring the detector to a circuit of its own, in order better to protect his family in the event of an electrical fire."

Other warning cases are more in the nature of informed-consent actions, where the plaintiff contends that he should have been warned of a danger in order to enable him to decide whether or not to purchase or use the product.  The plaintiff in Borel v. Fibreboard Paper Products Corp. (1973) asserted that he should have been warned of the danger of asbestos exposure.  Agreeing, the court said the "rationale for this rule is that the user or consumer is entitled to make his own choice as to whether the product's utility or benefits justify exposing himself to the risk of harm.  Thus, a true choice situation arises, and a duty to warn attaches, whenever a reasonable man would want to be informed of the risk in order to decide whether to expose himself to it." The plaintiff in Reyes v. Wyeth Labs. (1974) was entitled to be warned of the risk of contracting polio from ingesting defendant's Sabin vaccine containing a live polio virus. The warning would enable a user to decide whether or not "to be inoculated with killed-virus Salk vaccine, either to provide complete immunity or as a precautionary prelude to ingesting oral vaccine."

The informed-consent rationale may dictate the giving of a warning even though the warning might result in defendant's product being unacceptable to many or most users. This presumably would be the result had a proper warning been given in Wells v. Ortho Pharmaceutical Corp. (1986). There the court affirmed a judgment of $4,736,000 against the defendant for failure to warn the plaintiff that its spermicide contraceptive could act as a teratogen in the event that conception occurred while she was using the contraceptive.

Plaintiff has the burden of showing that, had a warning been given, it would have caused her to avoid the accident. In Sheehan v. Pima County (1982), the court held a jury could find that plaintiff failed to prove that knowledge of the danger of contracting polio from taking Sabin vaccine would have affected her conduct, since no Salk vaccine was available as an alternative and the risk of contracting polio from the Sabin vaccine was one out of five million.  In Conti v. Ford Motor Co. (1984), the court held that plaintiff failed as a matter of law to show that the presence of additional warnings would have prevented him from turning the ignition key without disengaging the clutch while his car was in reverse gear.  His action caused the car to lurch backward and injure his wife who was entering the car at the time. Plaintiff testified that he was "not paying attention to what he was doing when he started the car without disengaging the clutch," so there was "absolutely no evidence that additional warnings would have made any difference."  In Greiner v. Volkswagenwerk Aktiengesellschaft (1977), the court held that a warning about the high center of gravity of defendant's car would have made no difference in an emergency roll-over situation, and plaintiff's suggestion that the driver might not have bought the car had such a warning been given was unsupported by the evidence and based on "pure conjecture or guess."

Where the plaintiff failed to read the warning that was given, the court in E.R. Squibb & Sons, Inc. v. Cox (1985) held that the plaintiff cold not complain that a warning with clearer or stronger content would have made a difference.  However, if the plaintiff asserts that the defendant failed to use a reasonably effective way of communicating the warning, then failure to read the warning as given may not bar recovery.  The jury can reasonably infer that a better communicated warning might have been read. Rhodes v. Interstate Battery System of America, Inc. (1984).

The plaintiff in Thomas v. Hoffman–LaRoche, Inc. (1992) failed to establish a cause of action where her doctor testified that he would have prescribed defendant's acne medication even if warned of the possibility of seizures. But in Hibbs v. Abbott Laboratories (1991) the court said the mere fact that a doctor relied on his own scientific knowledge in prescribing DES did not prove that he would have ignored a warning by the drug manufacturer had one been given.

A warning is not required for a danger that is obvious, but as with cases of defective design the question of what is an obvious danger is not always an easy one. A plaintiff using charcoal briquettes might be unaware of the danger of asphyxiation, absent an adequate warning of the danger that could result from insufficient ventilation. Johnson v. Husky Industries, Inc. (1976). In Fraust v. Swift and Co. (1985), plaintiff sued a peanut butter manufacturer for failure to warn the mother of a 16–month–old child of the danger that the child could choke and suffer severe brain damage from eating peanut butter spread on bread. The court could not say "as a matter of law that the danger of a sixteen-month-old choking on a peanut butter sandwich is generally known and recognized."

Although there may be no general common law duty to warn of the dangers of alcohol consumption, Joseph E. Seagram and Sons v. McGuire

(1991), a duty may exist to warn of special dangers. Thus in Hon v. Stroh Brewery Co. (1987) the court held that a beer manufacturer could be required to warn of the risk of pancreatitis from consuming moderate amounts of beer. In Brune v. Brown Forman Corp. (1988) the court said a defendant manufacturer could be liable for failure to warn plaintiff's deceased of the risk of acute alcohol poisoning from consuming a number of straight shots of defendant's tequila over the course of an evening.

A duty to give a warning of generally known dangers may be imposed by statute, as in the federal cigarette labeling act, 15 U.S.C. § 1334, and the federal alcoholic beverage labeling act, 27 U.S.C. § 215. Violation of these statutes could constitute negligence per se, although a plaintiff would likely be met with a defense of assumption of the risk.

Sometimes expert testimony is required to determine the adequacy of warnings to a specialized group, such as to doctors, Hill v. Squibb & Sons, E.R. (1979), or to the medical community, Dion v. Graduate Hosp. of Univ. of Pa. (1987). For the most part, however, the adequacy of product warnings to lay persons is a matter that a lay jury can determine without the aid of expert testimony. In this respect warning cases differ significantly from design cases in general, where expert testimony as to design adequacy is usually required.

## 2.   THE STANDARD OF LIABILITY

There is a substantial division of authority regarding whether a negligence or strict liability standard is to be used in failure to warn cases. As the court said in Nesselrode v. Executive Beechcraft, Inc. (1986):

> The commentary accompanying Section 402A which pertains to failure to warn cases would seem to sanction the imposition of liability only when the defendant has knowledge or should have knowledge of the product's dangerous propensities. See Comment *j* to Section 402A. Some of the leading commentators also espouse the view that the successful maintenance of a Section 402A failure to warn action requires a showing of negligence. . . .   A substantial number of courts also take this position.

The *Nesselrode* court chose to follow a significant number of courts that impose strict liability in warning cases, and gave the following reasons for doing so:

> Strict tort liability recognizes that in today's world consumers can do little to protect themselves from the risk of serious injury caused by defects in the products they purchase. And, the more complex the product, the less opportunity there is for the consumer to guard against deleterious defects. To this extent, the consumer must rely upon the integrity and competency of the business community.   History, however, has

taught us that negligence liability alone provides an inadequate tort remedy for injured consumers and does little to stimulate greater care in the manufacturing process. Strict tort liability is rooted in these realities.

The imposition of strict tort liability is justified on the grounds that the manufacturer or seller is almost always better equipped than the consumer to endure the economic consequences of accidents caused by defective products. Everything in the marketplace has a price, including profits. Economic responsibility for the debilitating consequences of injuries caused by defective products is but one of the many costs associated with doing business and earning profits. All things considered, we find no unfairness in holding manufacturers and sellers economically and socially responsible for injuries actually caused by the products they place for profit in the stream of commerce.

The New Jersey Supreme Court in Beshada v. Johns–Manville Products Corp. (1982) gave additional reasons for applying strict liability principles in warning cases, and for rejecting the so-called "state of the art" defense:

The "state-of-the-art" at a given time is partly determined by how much industry invests in safety research. By imposing on manufacturers the costs of failure to discover hazards, we create an incentive for them to invest more actively in safety research.... The vast confusion that is virtually certain to arise from any attempt to deal in a trial setting with the concept of scientific knowability constitutes a strong reason for avoiding the concept altogether by striking the state-of-the-art defense.

Scientific knowability, as we understand it, refers not to what in fact was known at the time, but to what could have been known at the time. In other words, even if no scientist had actually formed the belief that asbestos was dangerous, the hazards would be deemed "knowable" if a scientist could have formed that belief by applying research or performing tests that were available at the time. Proof of what could have been known will inevitably be complicated, costly, confusing and time consuming. Each side will have to produce experts in the history of science and technology to speculate as to what knowledge was feasible in a given year. We doubt that juries will be capable of even understanding the concept of scientific knowability, much less be able to resolve such a complex issue. Moreover, we should resist legal rules that will so greatly add to the cost both sides incur in trying a case.

The concept of knowability is complicated further by the fact, noted above, that the level of investment in safety research by manufacturers is one determinant of the state-of-the-art at any given time. Fairness suggests that manufacturers not be excused from liability because their prior inadequate investment in safety rendered the hazards of their product unknowable. Thus, a judgment will have to be made as to whether defendants' investment in safety research in the years preceding distribution of the product was adequate. If not, the experts in the history of technology will have to testify as to what would have been knowable at the time of distribution if manufacturers had spent the proper amount on safety in prior years. To state the issue is to fully understand the great difficulties it would engender in a courtroom.

In a later case, Feldman v. Lederle Labs. (1984) (tetracycline antibiotic), the New Jersey court adopted a warning standard of "reason to know" for unavoidably unsafe products. There defendant contended "there was no scientific evidence" that its product "would cause tooth discoloration and such knowledge did not come into existence until after [plaintiff] had already ingested enough of the antibiotic to cause her problem."

The court in Graham v. Pittsburgh Corning Corp. (1990) applied a negligence standard in determining the duty to warn, but held that the duty may arise once a possibility, as opposed to a probability, of injury exists. In Shanks v. Upjohn Co. (1992) the court held that a manufacturer is strictly liable for failure to warn, "unless the defendant manufacturer can prove that the risk was scientifically unknowable at the time the product was distributed to the plaintiff."

In Halphen v. Johns-Manville Sales Corp. (1984) the court drew a distinction between foreseeability of risk (the product's inherent danger) and foreseeability of injury (the product's manner of use). Foreseeability of risk is assumed in a strict liability failure-to-warn case, the court said, although foreseeability of use may still be an issue. See *Newman v. Utility Trailer & Equip. Co., Inc.*, Chp. VII.B.1.

The court in Ayers v. Johnson & Johnson Baby Products Co. (1991) held that the parents of a child who suffered irreparable brain damage after aspirating baby oil were entitled to recover against the manufacturer of the oil for failure to warn of the danger. Under the applicable state statute, the plaintiffs were not required to prove foreseeability of harm, but only the likelihood and seriousness of the harm arising from failure to warn.

The warning cases are concerned with the issue of the knowability of danger, or of a method of preventing danger, at the time of manufacture, in deciding whether negligence of strict liability should apply. The plaintiff in all events must normally show knowability or preventability as of the time of trial.

Rule 407 of the Fed. Rules of Evid. permits "evidence of subsequent remedial measures" to show the "feasibility of precautionary measures". This rule supports the standard of strict liability in *Nesselrode* and *Beshada*.

The state-of-the-art standard is usually defined in terms of the scientific or technological knowledge available at a given time, while the negligence standard of due care is defined in terms of what a person knew, had reason to know, or should have known regarding a danger and the means of avoiding it. These two standards are not necessarily the same, even for a manufacturer with assumed expert knowledge in the field, since the reasonable person cannot always be expected to know that which is in fact knowable.

As noted in the previous chapter on design defects, a number of courts hold that evidence of industry custom is relevant to show scientific or technological feasibility, or state of the art. Where evidence of custom is admitted to prove state of the art, the standard becomes indistinguishable from negligence—whether for warning or for design.

### 3. PERSONS TO BE REACHED

Generally an expert need not be warned of dangers commonly associated with the use of products about which he has expert knowledge. There may be specific dangers of which the expert is unaware, however, and for which a warning will be required. A jury could find that a skilled electrician, said the court in Howard v. General Cable Corp. (1982), might be unaware of the danger of arcing and the lack of insulation on an aerial lift truck bucket.

The cases differ as to whether an employer's knowledge of a danger will relieve the manufacturer of a duty to warn the employer's employees, and the cases in this area are very fact-specific. In York v. Union Carbide Corp. (1992) the court held that the bulk supplier of argon gas had no duty to warn the employees of a steel manufacturer, which was a sophisticated purchaser of the product. Accord, Smith v. Walter C. Best, Inc. (1990) (no warning required to employees of silica sand purchaser). By contrast, the court in Brown v. Caterpillar Tractor Co. (1984) held that the Army's knowledge of the danger involved in operating a bulldozer without appropriate protective devices could not be imputed to an Army reserve member who was injured in such an operation.

Comment *n* to Rest. 2d of Torts § 388, dealing with the question of when a duty arises to warn the user directly regarding dangers associated with chattels furnished to third persons, states that the "magnitude of the risk involved must be compared with the burden" of requiring a direct warning. The risk's magnitude "is determined not only by the chance that some harm may result but also the serious or trivial character of the harm which is likely to result."

In Aluminum Co. of America v. Alm (1990) the court found that the defendant designer of a bottle cap closure system inadequately warned the consumer of the danger of a cap blow-off from faulty closure performance. The court also said that the bottler was not "an appropriate intermediary through which [the defendant] could have discharged its duty to warn the ultimate consumer". Similarly, in Sliman v. Aluminum Co. of America (1986), the court held that the defendant bottle cap manufacturer had a duty to warn of the danger of cap blow-offs from using tools to remove the bottle caps which were secured by "pilfer-proof" aluminum bands. Defendant Alcoa had knowledge of 229 previous injuries resulting from such attempts at removal. It "could have suggested or even insisted on a warning by the intermediaries. In addition, Alcoa could have communicated a warning through national media."

Comment *n* to Rest. 2d of Torts § 388 states that many articles

> can be made to carry their own message to the understanding of those who are likely to use them by the form in which they are put out, by the container in which they are supplied, or by a label or other device, indicating with a substantial sufficiency their dangerous character. Where the danger involved in the ignorant use of their true quality is great and such means of disclosure are practicable and not unduly burdensome, it may well be that the supplier should be required to adopt them.

In Brizendine v. Visador Co. (1970), the court held that the defendant glass company had a duty to warn all persons in the chain of distribution that its glass was unsuitable for use in high traffic areas. A warning sticker on the glass might have fulfilled this duty, the court said. The manufacturer of a wire rope sling did not fulfill its duty by warning plaintiff's employer of the rated capacity of the sling, said the court in West v. Broderick & Bascom Rope Co. (1972). The evidence showed that the danger of injury from breakage of the sling was substantial, and that "without great burden, a curved tag, which would not likely be knocked off in service, could be bonded to a depression in the collar of each sling."

It is generally held that there is no duty to warn a patient of dangers associated with prescription drugs, since a warning to the prescribing doctor is sufficient. Johnson v. American Cyanamid Co. (1986) (oral polio vaccine). The doctor is the consumer for purposes of determining consumer expectations and risk-utility in this context, Shanks v. Upjohn Co. (1992). In Swayze v. McNeil Labs., Inc. (1987), however, the court held that an anesthetic manufacturer had no duty to take any action to prevent the nonsupervision by doctors of nurse anesthetists during surgery, even though this practice was well known to the medical community, since the prescribing doctors were sufficiently warned of the danger.

The so-called "learned intermediary" rule for prescription drugs, whereby only the doctor need be warned, may be in a process of change. In the case of prescription birth control pills, the court in MacDonald v. Ortho Pharmaceutical Corp. (1985) held that a warning had to be given directly to the consumer by package insert. Whereas the patient's involvement in decision-making concerning the use of prescription drugs is normally minimal, "the healthy, young consumer of oral contraceptives is usually actively involved in the decision to use 'the pill'—and the prescribing physician is relegated to a relatively passive role."  Contra, Reaves v. Ortho Pharmaceutical Corp. (1991) ("patients are unlikely to understand technical medical information regarding the nature and propensities of oral contraceptives").

Where it is foreseeable, as in Reyes v. Wyeth Labs. (1974) (oral polio vaccine), that a drug will be administered without the intervention of a doctor as a learned intermediary, a warning by the manufacturer directly to the consumer may be required. But in Mazur v. Merck & Co. (1992) the court held that a nurse could act as a learned intermediary in administering a prescription vaccine during a measles epidemic, provided it was shown that the nurse was familiar with the vaccine package insert and carefully reviewed the medical record for each patient.

## 4.  COUNTERVAILING REPRESENTATIONS

Whether or not a warning might otherwise be adequate, it can be made inadequate by countervailing representations that downplay the danger or mislead the user regarding the nature or extent of the danger.  The mixing instructions for a cleaner in McCully v. Fuller Brush Co. (1966) were inadequate as a warning, and rendered more inadequate by the representation on the container that the product was "Kind To Your Hands." The caution on the cleaning fluid can in Maize v. Atlantic Ref. Co. (1945), stating, "Do not inhale fumes. Use only in well ventilated place", was counteracted by the conspicuous display of the words "Safety–Kleen" which were "so prominently featured as to exclude from [plaintiff's] mind that 'provident fear' which has been characterized as 'the mother of safety'."

Warnings by a drug manufacturer as to the possible side effects of its product were counteracted by the manufacturer's detail men, or salespersons, "who minimized the dangers of the drug while emphasizing its effectiveness, wide acceptance and use, and lack of certain objectionable side effects associated with other drugs," Incollingo v. Ewing (1971). A warning to keep empty the chamber under the hammer of a Colt .22 revolver, in Johnson v. Colt Industries (1986), was inadequate because it neither described the risk nor the possible consequences, and also because it was counteracted by other statements indicating that the gun could safely be kept fully loaded.

A warning may be neutralized by pictures or by appearances of safety. The toxicity of the cleaner in Jonescue v. Jewel Home Shop. Serv. (1973) was minimized by its container, a "white, plastic bottle with a red, white, blue and aqua label, lending to it a colorful and harmless appearance." The warnings of the danger of improper installation of a gas space heater, in Wallinger v. Martin Stamping and Stove Co. (1968), were undermined by a cutaway drawing of the heater in defendant's pamphlet showing a vent pipe not extending beyond the peak of the roof as required for safe ventilation. A highly toxic insecticide labeled as such could be confused with drinking water because it was contained in a clear gallon jug. Ziglar v. E.I. Du Pont De Nemours and Co. (1981). The warning against doubling on a motorbike, in Evridge v. American Honda Motor Co. (1985), was diluted by a design indicating a place for a passenger behind the driver.

The plaintiff may be required to show that the defendant's alleged overpromotion caused his injuries, Dauphin Deposit Bank and Trust Co. v. Toyota (1991), in order to recover on the basis of such overpromotion. In Smith v. Anheuser–Busch, Inc. (1991) the plaintiff was not entitled to recover based on advertising which allegedly caused the plaintiff to consume defendant's beer, become intoxicated, and suffer injuries as a result, since the plaintiff was unable to identify specific advertising on which he relied or to show how it could reasonably have affected his conduct.

It is apparent that a variety of circumstances surrounding the packaging, marketing and appearance of a product may serve to counteract any warnings that are given. These circumstances are in the nature of misrepresentations, for which strict liability may be imposed. The entire environment in which a product is marketed should be taken into account in judging the adequacy of warnings.

### 5.  POST–SALE DUTIES TO WARN

Where a defendant markets a defective and unreasonably dangerous product, it may have a post-sale duty to warn of dangers associated with the product. If the court, as in Bly v. Otis Elevator Co. (1983), holds that the duty to warn is based on negligence, then that duty might not arise until sometime after the product is sold—at a time when the seller knows or should know of the danger. A negligent failure to warn can exist at the time of sale also, of course, as can a duty based on strict liability. As noted in the section on statutes of limitations in Chapter IV, a continuing or subsequent duty to warn may toll the statute of limitations, although it has been held that such a tolling occurs only when the duty is one of due care, rather than strict liability. Brown v. Merrow Mach. Co. (1976).

While some courts have said that a post-sale or continuing duty to warn arises only if the product was defective when originally sold, such a holding is questionable. The court in Feldman v. Lederle Laboratories (1991) recognized a continuing duty to warn, as knowledge of the risks developed, regard-

ing the propensity of the drug tetracycline to dis-
color young children's teeth.

A continuing duty to warn may exist after the
plaintiff is no longer exposed to the product, since
a warning may enable the plaintiff to take preventive measures.   Lockwood v. A C & S, Inc. (1987).
A post-sale duty to warn may also continue even
after the defendant has stopped manufacturing the
product.   Owens–Illinois v. Zenobia (1992).

The post-sale duty may be greater than one of
just warning.   A duty to recall may be imposed by
statute, as under the Nat. Traffic and Motor Vehicle Safety Act.   A duty to repair may also be imposed by common law decision, where it appears
likely that a warning will be ineffective.   Such a
duty was found to exist in Balido v. Improved
Machinery, Inc. (1972), where the employer-pur-
chaser failed to heed defendant's warning to install
a necessary safety device on a product that injured
the plaintiff-employee.   In Gracyalny v. Westinghouse Electric Corp. (1983), the court found that
the defendant could be held to a post-sale duty not
only to supply a needed safety component part, but
also to install the part where there was a substantial risk of improper and dangerous installation by
the purchaser.

In situations where corporation B buys the business of corporation A, and B then continues to
operate that business in essentially the same way
as A did, B may or may not be vicariously liable for
injuries resulting from defective products sold by A

before it sold the business to B. The liability of the successor corporation in this situation depends on the law of de facto merger which differs from jurisdiction to jurisdiction as discussed in Chapter III.

Whether or not the successor is vicariously liable for injuries caused by defective products sold by the predecessor, the successor may nevertheless owe a duty to warn of dangers associated with products sold by the predecessor. Schumacher v. Richards Sheer Co., Inc. (1983). This duty can arise where the successor services accounts of the predecessor and becomes aware of the danger.

In Polius v. Clark Equip. Co. (1986), the court indicated that such a duty did not arise where the successor did not succeed to the predecessor's service contracts, had no actual knowledge of the alleged defect, and no business relation with the plaintiff's employer. In Downtowner, Inc. v. Acrometal Products, Inc. (1984), the court said:

> The common thread running through these decisions imposing an independent duty to warn upon a successor corporation is the establishment of a relationship between the successor and its predecessor's customers.... Various factors have been considered to establish this nexus, for example: where the successor had inherited the service contracts which included responsibility for servicing the defective product; coverage of the particular product under the service contract; service of the product by the successor;

and the successor's knowledge of the location and owner of the machine.... This listing cannot be said to be exhaustive. Rather than relying upon specific factors, the courts appear to have employed a risk/benefit analysis to determine whether it would be just to impose such a duty.

In the *Schumacher* case, supra, the court indicated that the duty to warn could arise as a result of the successor's knowledge of the "location and owner" of the product, a single service call and offers of further service, the successor's holding itself out "as having expertise in the product line," and a showing that the successor "knew or had reason to know" of the danger.

A successor corporation's duty to warn can arise, of course, even where the successor is also vicariously liable under the doctrine of de facto merger. A plaintiff is normally allowed to sue on as many theories of recovery as she can establish, and a warning claim may be a valuable additional basis where the facts establishing merger are doubtful, or where some defense such as the statute of limitations may be applicable to the merger claim but not to the claim of failure to warn.

## 6. ALLERGIC USERS

The only duty normally owed to allergic users is one of warning, and then only when the plaintiff is a member of a substantial or appreciable number of persons subject to the allergy, where the defendant should have known of this risk.    Adelman–Tremblay v. Jewel Companies, Inc. (1988).    There is no precise definition of what constitutes a substantial or appreciable number, and in one case 373 complaints out of 82 million sales were held to be sufficient.    Wright v. Carter Products, Inc. (1957).    If the defendant makes an express warranty as to the safety of its product, then the defense of an allergic reaction may be unavailable.    Drake v. Charles of Fifth Ave., Inc. (1970).

Comment *j* to Rest. 2d of Torts § 402A states that the "seller may reasonably assume that those with common allergies, as for example to eggs or strawberries, will be aware of them, and he is not required to warn against them."    The seller, however, may be required to warn that his product contains eggs, or peanut butter, or indeed any other ingredient that is a known allergen.    The seller may also have to warn of the symptoms associated with an allergic reaction, and in the case of cosmetics to warn of the necessity of performing a patch test before each use where such a test is effective.    D'Arienzo v. Clairol, Inc. (1973).

## B.    MISREPRESENTATIONS

As discussed in Chapter II, an action for misrepresentation can arise in a variety of contexts.    The misrepresentation can be based on deceit, negligence, strict tort, or strict warranty.    No defect

need be shown, other than the fact that the misrepresentation was made and proximately caused the
plaintiff's injury.   Huebert v. Federal Pac. Elec.
Co. (1972).   A misrepresentation may arise from
the appearance of the product itself.   Hochberg v.
O'Donnell's Restaurant, Inc. (1971).   The decisions
vary regarding the necessity of proving reliance,
and regarding the effect of reliance on the bargaining and user process.

Where strict liability for misrepresentation is
imposed—based either on warranty or tort—a
number of product defenses and liability limitations can be avoided.   The product supplier who
makes an innocent misrepresentation may not be
able to rely on a state-of-the-art defense.   It may be
irrelevant that the defendant is allergic to the
product, that the product is used, or that there is a
statutory protection (as in the case of blood and
blood products) from implied strict liability.   A
misrepresentation can toll the statute of limitations, and it can prevent a disclaimer of liability
from being effective.   As noted in the preceding
section, a misrepresentation can neutralize the effect of a warning.   These and other attributes of an
action based on misrepresentation make it a potent
basis of liability in products litigation.

# CHAPTER VII

# PROBLEMS OF PROOF

## A. CAUSE–IN–FACT

### 1. IN GENERAL

Plaintiff generally must show not only that defendant's product was defective and that the defect caused his injuries, but he must also show that the defect existed when the product left the defendant's control. For this purpose, he must reasonably eliminate alternative causes not attributable to the defendant. Having done so, he need not identify the precise defect that caused his injury. Where a defect attributable to the defendant is established, courts may be more willing to allow an inference of causation than they would if no such defect is shown.

In Browder v. Pettigrew (1976), the court held a jury question was presented as to the existence of a manufacturing defect which caused the A-frame supporting the right front wheel of plaintiffs' automobile to collapse, resulting in personal injuries and property damage. The car was only two to three weeks old, plaintiffs had had no previous trouble with it, and it had not been damaged in any way prior to the accident. The court quoted with approval Scanlon v. General Motors Corp. (1974):

As a rule the mere occurrence of an accident is not sufficient to establish that the product was not fit for ordinary purposes. However, additional circumstantial evidence, such as proof of proper use, handling or operation of the product and the nature of the malfunction, may be enough to establish the requirement that something is wrong with it.

The newer the product, the better able the plaintiff will be to make out a submissible case based on circumstantial evidence of defect, where there are no likely intervening causes. In Anderson v. Chrysler Corp. (1991) the plaintiff established a case by circumstantial evidence where his relatively new car had undergone numerous repairs for electrical problems including one the day before a fire broke out under the dashboard. By contrast, the plaintiff in Kourouvacilis v. General Motors Corp. (1991) presented no evidence to show that the 1985 fire in her 1979 car was caused by a defect in the wiring traceable to the manufacturer. Even if the product is relatively new when an accident occurs, the plaintiff may lose if she cannot eliminate reasonably likely alternative causes. Roselli v. General Electric Co. (1991) (one-year-old glass coffee pot shattered, misuse not reasonably eliminated as cause).

Dickson v. National Supermarkets, Inc. (1987), illustrates how a combination of circumstantial evidence and expert testimony may be necessary to make out a submissible case. Five family members all became sick after eating some "gooey butter cake" sold by the defendant. The family had "no other food in common that day" except the cake, and an expert diagnosed "plaintiffs as having food poisoning." This evidence was held sufficient to establish a prima facie case against the defendant.

There have been a number of cases involving the amount of proof necessary to justify an inference of causation in asbestos cases. The problem here is the long latency period of the attendant diseases, combined with the fact that the types of diseases involved including various kinds of cancer are not caused solely by asbestos. Recovery often depends on the frequency of use of the defendant's product, and the regularity and extent of the plaintiff's exposure thereto. Wehmeier v. UNR Industries (1991). Epidemiological evidence, combined with expert testimony relating plaintiff's colon cancer to his particular physiology, was held sufficient in Grassis v. Johns–Manville Corp. (1991). Plaintiff's mere presence at various jobsites where defendant's product was used may however be insufficient to establish causation. Benshoof v. National Gypsum Co. (1991). Similarly, the evidence may be insufficient where plaintiff's exposure to the defendant's product was relatively slight compared to exposure to the products of others. Fiffick v. GAF Corp. (1992).

Where a defect attributable to the defendant is reasonably established by the proof, the courts appear more prone than they would be otherwise to allow the causation question to go to the jury. In Campbell v. General Motors Corp. (1982), the 62–year–old plaintiff alleged a design defect in the absence of a handrail or guardrail on the bus in front of the first seat where she was sitting, so that when the bus suddenly stopped she was thrown forward onto the floor and injured as a result. The court found a jury question was presented as to whether the ordinary consumer would consider the absence of such a handrail to be a design defect.

On the issue of whether the absence of a handrail caused the accident—or whether the presence of a handrail would have prevented the accident—the court said:

The plaintiff in a strict liability action is not required to disprove every possible alternative explanation of the injury in order to have the case submitted to the jury. "It is not incumbent upon a plaintiff to show that an inference in his favor is the only one that may be reasonably drawn from the evidence; he need only show that the material fact to be proved may logically and reasonably be inferred from the circumstantial evidence.... The mere fact that other inferences adverse to plaintiff might be drawn does not render the inference favorable to plaintiff too conjectural or speculative for consideration [by the jury]"....

It is particularly appropriate that the jury be allowed to determine the inference to be drawn when the evidence indicates that a safety device, designed to prevent the very injury that occurred, was not present. To take the case from the jury simply because the plaintiff could not prove to a certainty that the device would have prevented the accident would enable the manufacturer to prevail on the basis of its failure to provide the safeguard....

Under these principles, the evidence introduced by plaintiff in the present case was sufficient to withstand the motion for nonsuit. Plaintiff testified that she was injured when thrown from her seat to the floor on the opposite side of the bus. She further testified that before falling she reached out with both arms for something to hold on to, but nothing was there. Given plaintiff's position at the time the bus turned, a jury could reasonably infer from the evidence that a handrail or guardrail within her reach would have prevented the accident. Although this fact may not be capable of mathematical proof, it is nevertheless a reasonable inference that may be drawn from the evidence.

In Bettencourt v. Pride Well Service, Inc. (1987), plaintiff, who had been drinking before going to work, suffered severe injuries when he fell from the top of defendants' oil tanks, where he was required to work at night by flashlight. The top of the tanks "was smeared with oil and was slippery", and the "ladder for ascending and descending the first tank had only one handhold at the top on the left side which consisted of a four-inch pipe which was difficult to grip." Plaintiff suffered traumatic amnesia from the fall and was unable to remember the accident. Citing cases where the intestate unexplainably drowned because of the absence of a sufficiently buoyant heaving line or the absence of a lifeguard, and where the plaintiff inexplicably fell down steps "which had loose edges and protruding nails," the court found that the "circumstantial evidence here present and common knowledge provide a basis from which the causal sequence can be inferred."

In warning cases the necessary proof of causation may be attenuated. For example, in Campos v. Firestone Tire & Rubber Co. (1984) the plaintiff, a Portuguese emigrant employee, was severely injured when he inserted his hand into the cage where a tire was being inflated on a three-piece rim. During the inflation plaintiff saw the lock-ring component of the rim assembly separating; and, fearing there would be "a very big accident" if the pieces separated under pressure, he reached into the cage to disengage the hose from the tire. The rim exploded while he was reaching into the cage, and he was injured as a result.

Plaintiff had received written and oral instructions regarding the danger involved, and he had had a similar accident six years previously. His expert "suggested that defendant should have produced a graphic or symbolic warning against inserting one's hand in the protective cage during the inflation process.... He testified that the manufacturer should have anticipated that illiterate people would be exposed to these dangers." While the court found that plaintiff "made little, if any, showing that with a proper warning the accident would not have occurred," it nevertheless remanded the case for a new trial on the warning issue. In doing so, it noted that "in failure to warn cases some courts have helped plaintiffs overcome the burden of proof by positing a rebuttable presumption that the warning would have been heeded if given."

Causation of damages can be inferred when their likelihood is within the realm of common knowledge. In Gentry v. Stokely–Van Camp (1982), the plaintiff discovered a condom in a can of defendant's pork and beans that he was eating, and he alleged "a loss of appetite, a revulsion for pork and beans, mental anguish, and difficulty in eating and retaining food since the incident." In affirming a $2500 judgment for the plaintiff, the appellate court said: "We think nausea and vomiting as a result of eating contaminated food does not require medical proof" to permit an inference of causation, and "a reasonable mind could infer" causation from "the eating and sight of something as repulsive as a condom in a can of pork and beans."

A plaintiff may also be able to recover under a res ipsa loquitur approach to proof of causation.

The plaintiff truck driver in Bradshaw v. Freight-liner Corp. (1991) was entitled to a res ipsa instruction as to the manufacturer of a truck seat that was properly installed and well maintained. The seat rubbed against a shock absorber, causing the seat's air bag to collapse when the driver hit a hole.

There are some cases in which plaintiff's proof of harm is less than a preponderance, and plaintiff has been permitted to recover a fraction of his damages proportional to the amount by which his risk of injury is increased by the chance of harm. Also, in toxic injuries, plaintiff is often unable to show that his injury was more probably than not caused by defendant's toxin, but can only show an epidemiologically increased risk to the general population that was exposed to the toxin. There is substantial commentary and some case law support for allowing recovery based on such epidemiological proof.

## 2.  SEVERAL POSSIBLE CAUSES

There are two common fact patterns where the conduct of more than one at-fault actor may combine to cause an injury. The first is where only one of the actors actually caused the injury. In this situation, Rest. 2d of Torts § 433B(3) shifts the burden of proof to the actors to show they were not the cause. The second is where the conduct of two or more at-fault actors actually contributed to the injury, but the extent of their contribution is unclear. In this situation, Rest. 2d of Torts § 433B(2) shifts the burden of proof to the actors to show the extent of their contribution to the cause. In either situation, actors who are unable to carry this burden will be liable for all of the damages attributable to the multiple actors.

Another approach to these situations is to allow the plaintiff to recover in full if he can show that the defendant's conduct was likely a substantial, as opposed to a but-for, cause of the plaintiff's injury. In re Manguno (1992). This approach may be followed even if one of the likely causes is not a suable person. Dale v. Baltimore & O.R. Co. (1986).

The famous two-fires case, Anderson v. Minneapolis, St. P. & S.S.M. Ry. (1920), would allow recovery in full against a tortfeasor where his conduct combines with that of another cause, whether or not that other cause is suable, and whether or not the proof shows that any of the causes alone was sufficient to cause the entire injury. The principle of this case is embodied in Rest. 2d of Torts § 432(2) ("two forces . . . actively operating").

If defendants engage in a conspiracy to conceal a tort, they may be jointly and severally liable for resulting injury even though the product of only one of the defendants caused the injury. In Nicolet, Inc. v. Nutt (1987), the appellate court affirmed the trial court in holding that plaintiffs stated a cause of action against a manufacturer whose product did not cause plaintiffs' purported injury, where the manufacturer allegedly conspired with other asbestos manufacturers to intentionally misrepresent and suppress information concerning the health hazards of asbestos. The trial court in this case, in In re Asbestos Litigation (1986), defined the type of conduct necessary to create a tortious conspiracy:

"Knowing participation" in a conspiracy, however, need not be an express agreement; tacit ratification is sufficient.... The District Court for Delaware has stated that even membership and knowledge of the association's wrongful conduct is not, by itself, sufficient to show "knowing participation," but once that is coupled with a consistent later act, an inference of knowing participation is permissible.... Likewise, consciously parallel action is not sufficient to show conspiracy, but it is enough that knowing concerted action was contemplated or invited, the defendant adhered to the scheme and participated in it.

The conspiracy or concert of action theory was used as a basis for imposing joint liability against diethystilbestrol (DES) manufacturers in Abel v. Eli Lilly and Co. (1984). Where this theory is sustained, it is immaterial whether the defendant whose product actually caused the injury is identified or not. Plaintiffs stated a cause of action by alleging that the "defendants acted together in negligently manufacturing and promoting drugs which were ineffective and dangerous, were inadequately tested, and were distributed without sufficient warnings."

In Hall v. E.I. Du Pont (1972), the court held that joint liability could be imposed against the manufacturers of blasting caps for failure to warn of the danger associated with the use of such caps. Here the defendants through their trade association had joint control of the risk, and they made a collective decision not to warn of the danger.

In Holliday v. Peden (1978), the plaintiff was injured when a surgical needle broke in his throat during a tonsillectomy. The court said the evidence established that the needle broke "as a result of either of three causes, i.e., the negligent handling of the needle by hospital personnel, the defective manufacture of the needle, or the application of too much stress on the needle by the surgeon." In this situation, plaintiff need not show any concert of action on the part of the defendant hospital, manufacturer, and doctor. The *Holliday* principle was applied in Anderson v. Somberg (1975) (rongeur broke in plaintiff's spine during laminectomy), where a doctor and hospital were sued in negligence and the product distributor and manufacturer in strict liability. Since "all parties had been joined who could reasonably have been connected" with negligent use of, or a defect in, the product, the court held that the jury had to find at least one of the defendants liable. The court followed *Anderson* in McGuinness v. Wakefern Corp. (1991) (salmonella contracted from one of five different ingredients used in preparing lasagna).

The drug DES, (diethystilbestrol) has generated extensive litigation throughout the country. Administered as an antiabortifacient from 1947 to 1971, the drug has been found to cause cervical cancer in the female offspring of the mothers who took it, and in Pine v. Eli Lilly & Co. (1985) it was alleged that the drug caused testicular cancer in the male offspring of such mothers. The product was sold over-the-counter as a generic drug, with the manufacturer not identified. When the offspring manifested cancer symptoms many years after their mothers had ingested the drug, it proved impossible to identify the manufacturer whose drug actually caused the individual plaintiff's injury.

Unwilling to leave the injured plaintiff remediless in this situation, but also unwilling to hold the defendants jointly liable, the court in Sindell v. Abbott Labs. (1980) devised the market-share-liability doctrine, which has been followed in several other jurisdictions. See Smith v. Eli Lilly & Co. (1990) (rejecting the doctrine, reviewing cases pro and con); Conley v. Boyle Drug Co. (1990) (adopting doctrine, but limiting its application to negligence). Under this doctrine, the *Sindell* court said, the plaintiff was required to join as defendants "the manufacturers of a substantial share of the DES which her mother might have taken", and then the burden of proof shifted to the defendants "to demonstrate that they could not have made the substance which injured plaintiff." Each defendant that is unable to carry this burden "will be held liable for the proportion of the judgment represented by its share of that market." The court found it "reasonable in the present context to measure the likelihood that any of the defendants supplied the product which allegedly injured plaintiff by the percentage which the DES sold by each of them for the purpose of preventing miscarriage bears to the entire production of the drug sold by all for the purpose."

It has been held that the *Sindell* doctrine should not be applied when the plaintiff can identify a defendant who actually caused his injury. Zafft v. Eli Lilly & Co. (1984); contra, Hymowitz v. Eli Lilly & Co. (1989) (no defense to prove lack of causation). Even when the doctrine applies, the *Sindell* case leaves uncertain what percentage of the manufacturers that represent the total market must be joined as defendants, and how the market apportionment among defendants is to be made. In George v. Parke–Davis (1987), the court held that data for the narrowest market possible should be used in determining the market share of a defendant. "Thus, in this case, in which the plaintiff's mother allegedly purchased the DES in one pharmacy in Idaho, that particular pharmacy should be the relevant market." In *Hymowitz v. Eli Lilly & Co.*, supra, on the other hand, the court used a national market to determine market share.

Not all courts follow the *Sindell* approach. Some reject it altogether, as in *Smith v. Eli Lilly & Co.*, supra, leaving the plaintiff remediless when she is unable to identify the defendant whose product actually caused her injury. The Wisconsin court in Collins v. Eli Lilly Co. (1984) used fault-related criteria for apportioning liability among defendants. In making the apportionment of liability, the jury should consider

> whether the drug company conducted tests on DES for safety and efficacy in use for pregnancies, to what degree the company took a role in gaining FDA approval of DES for use in pregnancies; whether the company had a small or large market share in the relevant area; whether the company took the lead or merely followed the lead of others in producing or marketing DES; whether the company issued warnings about the dangers of DES; whether the company produced or marketed DES after it knew or should have known of the possible hazards DES presented to the public; and whether the company took any affirmative steps to reduce the risk of injury to the public. This list of factors is not exclusive, and the trial court may in its discretion permit the jury to consider other factors relevant to apportioning liability.

Some courts have rejected the market-share basis of liability for similar products that have varying degrees of harmfulness, on the ground that the market-proportion rationale is inapplicable since the proportion of the market sold does not necessarily reflect the proportion of injuries likely caused by a defendant. Vigiolto v. Johns–Manville Corp. (1986).

In Sheffield v. Eli Lilly & Co. (1983), the court held that an injury sustained from a deviant defective Salk vaccine furnished no basis for imposing market-share liability against Salk vaccine manufacturers. This situation, said the court, differed from the DES cases where the whole industry was at fault. But in Doe v. Cutter Biological, Inc. (1992) the court applied market share liability in favor of plaintiffs who contracted AIDS after receiving a blood-clotting agent manufactured by one of the four defendants. This case resembles *Anderson v. Somberg*, supra.

The court in Enright v. Eli Lilly & Co. (1991) held that a second-generation plaintiff could not recover for injuries resulting from her grandmother's ingestion of DES. The court denied recovery in this case as a policy matter, concluding that the line should be drawn in order to prevent unlimited liability in time.

# B. PROXIMATE CAUSE AND FORESEEABILITY
## 1. IN GENERAL

Sometimes courts speak of the absence of duty, the lack of proximate cause, and unforeseeability as if these terms were interchangeable, and often the meaning of one term does reinforce the other. To say, as in Higgc v. General Motors Corp. (1985), that a car unequipped with airbags is not defective because a consumer would "not expect air bags to pop out of the dash" can be translated to mean that there is no duty owed by the manufacturer, or that the absence of airbags was not a proximate cause of the accident, or that the occurrence of the accident owing to the absence of airbags was unforeseeable. Similarly, in Simpson v. Standard Container Co. (1987) the court held that the defendant was not liable for injuries to children caused by the spillage of gasoline from a heavy-duty gasoline can that lacked a child-proof cap, because the warnings on the side of the can ("Keep Out of Reach of Children" and "Do Not Store in Vehicle or Living Space") were adequate, and because the "can was not being used for the purpose and in a manner that was reasonably foreseeable."

Lear Siegler, Inc. v. Perez (1991) illustrates proximate cause analysis. There the plaintiffs' deceased, an employee of the state highway department, had pulled his truck to the side of the highway to attempt repair of a flashing arrow sign which he was towing. While thus stopped, he was struck and killed by another driver who had fallen asleep at the wheel.

Plaintiffs sued the sign manufacturer, contending that had the sign not malfunctioned the deceased "would not have been at the place where the collision occurred at the time it occurred."

The court considered "these particular circumstances" to be "too roughly connected" with the death of the deceased "to constitute legal cause," and sustained summary judgment for the defendant.

Compare General Motors Corp. v. Johnston (1992). There the plaintiff was permitted to recover for the death of her deceased caused by a defective memory chip in the deceased's pickup truck. The defect caused the pickup to stall, resulting in the deceased's death.

Often the concept of foreseeability is used to describe occurrences that can reasonably be anticipated, while proximate cause is used to describe occurrences that are the "direct", "natural" or "probable" result of another event. No bright line of distinction between the terms can be made on this basis, however. Occurrences that are fully anticipatable—such as injuries from obvious dangers, or from products that are dangerous as a matter of common knowledge—may be described as unforeseeable, while other occurrences that result from a complex chain of causation may nevertheless be described as proximately caused by a remote event in that chain. The terms therefore are treated in this section as they are usually treated by the courts, that is, as essentially synonymous.

In Newman v. Utility Trailer & Equip. Co., Inc. (1977), the court distinguished foreseeability of danger from foreseeability of use for purposes of strict liability.  In "strict liability the knowledge of the article's propensity to inflict harm as it did is assumed regardless of whether the manufacturer or seller foresaw or reasonably should have foreseen the danger."  But before "a manufacturer or other seller is strictly liable for injury inflicted by a product, the product must have been put to a foreseeable use."  In negligence, both the danger and the use of a product must be foreseeable, while only foreseeability of use is required in strict liability.  See *Halphen v. Johns–Manville Sales Corp.* (1984), Chp. VI.A.2.

Proximate cause questions are an admixture of cause-in-fact issues and policy questions.  Perhaps no area of products liability and tort law is more difficult to generalize about than proximate cause, and the subject can be appreciated only by example and with a recognition that the area is fact-specific and fluid.  In spite of the difficulty of meaningfully talking about proximate cause in general terms, the subject is nevertheless central to the functioning of a products and tort reparations system.  The idea of proximate cause expresses fundamental feelings of fairness and common sense that inhere in the common law system.

## 2.  MISUSE

Misuse is treated as an affirmative defense by some courts, and others place the burden on the plaintiff to show the absence of misuse as part of plaintiff's case-in-chief. Misuse is usually not treated as a bar to recovery unless it is considered unforeseeable. Unforeseeable misuse is a bar, while foreseeable misuse is not. Misuse, when attributable to the plaintiff rather than a third person, is closely related to contributory negligence and assumption of the risk, and these concepts will be further considered in the section below on plaintiff misconduct.

In Ellsworth v. Sherne Lingerie, Inc. (1985), the court recognized that decisions "are split on the question of whether the issue of misuse properly arises as part of the plaintiff's case, or is an affirmative defense." It noted that the "recent trend" has been to treat misuse "as a part of the plaintiff's case, and as being directly related to the issues of defectiveness, or of proximate cause, or of both." The court adopted this latter position, and defined misuse as "a use not reasonably foreseeable."

The plaintiff here was burned by an allegedly dangerously flammable nightgown which she was wearing inside out with two pockets protruding at hip level as she reached up to a cabinet over a lighted stove, setting the gown on fire. The court held as a matter of law that plaintiff's conduct was reasonably foreseeable.

It certainly may be foreseen that wearing apparel, such as nightgowns and robes, will occasionally be worn inside out. It is also foreseeable that a loosely fitting gown will come into contact with sources of ignition in the environment where it may be expected to be worn, and particularly when worn in the kitchen and near a stove. Momentary inattention or carelessness on the part of the user, while it may constitute contributory negligence, does not add up to misuse of the product under these circumstances.

In Bryan v. John Bean Div. of FMC Corp. (1978) the plaintiff was injured when defendant's "cast iron tool known as a clevis, used in bending an automobile axle for wheel alignment, broke into pieces under pressure, and one of the pieces struck plaintiff, causing loss of an eye and allegedly causing back injuries."  The jury found both a manufacturing defect (the clevis "contained a dangerous crack, high levels of porosity and impurity, and was overly brittle") and a design defect (the defendant furnished "inadequate specifications" for manufacture "leading to a product too hard and brittle, characteristics that contributed to propagation of a crack in the metal"). Defendant contended "that prior misuse and mishandling by employees of [plaintiff's employer] had made the clevis fragile and likely to break."  In finding the misuse defense presented a question for the jury, the court said:

> We question whether the misuse defense has as wide a scope in cases of manufacturing defect, which, by definition, present a flaw in the product not intended to occur.  In these circumstances, misuse relates only to causation of the

accident rather than tending to prove the absence of a defect in the product as manufactured.

The fact that the plaintiff is himself guilty of criminal conduct in his acquisition or use of a product will not necessarily bar his recovery on grounds of unforeseeable misuse, although such conduct may go to the issue of contributory negligence or assumption of the risk. Rest. 2d of Torts § 889. The 15–year–old plaintiff in Ashmore v. Cleanweld Products, Inc. (1983), was held to have stated a cause of action against the manufacturer and seller of an allegedly unreasonably dangerous product, even though plaintiff was using the product in the illegal manufacture of explosives at the time of injury. While the court recognized that "there is a strong public policy against the illegal manufacture of explosives," that policy "is best effectuated ... through penal laws." In Pegg v. General Motors Corp. (1978), on the other hand, the court in an equally divided opinion affirmed the trial court's decision that there was no duty owed to a thief by the manufacturer of an allegedly unreasonably dangerous chemical water sanitizer. Perhaps this decision can better be explained on the grounds that the plaintiff was an adult who was barred by his own contributory negligence.

The court in Falkenbury v. Elder Cadillac, Inc. (1982) held it was foreseeable that the plaintiff would injure himself on a sharp object while trying to eliminate a rattle inside the spoked wire wheel of a car manufactured and sold by the defendants.

It distinguished a case, Tibbetts v. Ford Motor Co. (1976), where recovery was denied on closely similar facts. The dissent contended that the majority was in effect holding that "a car is reasonably safe only if virtually every potentially sharp edge is trimmed with jewelry-like precision [and] the car is bedecked with warning stickers for each sharp edge which could remain." The majority pointed out that there was a spoke repair kit available, making it "reasonably foreseeable that the spokes might become loosened" and repair of the wheel cover might be undertaken by the owner.

*Falkenbury* should be contrasted with May v. Gillette Safety Razor Co. (1984). In *May* the appellate court affirmed the trial court's denial of relief based on a claim for injuries resulting from swallowing a razor blade manufactured by the defendant. Plaintiff contended there was a breach of express warranty because the blade was advertised as made of stainless steel, but "must have been of another material" since it "had not shown up on an x-ray." The court said it did "not consider the swallowing of a razor blade a risk which the defendant is required to anticipate," and it refused to remand "where, at most, only nominal damages could be recovered." The court did not explain under what bizarre circumstances the plaintiff managed to swallow the blade, or why the damages were only nominal.

Plaintiff's intentional misconduct may bar recovery. In Daniell v. Ford Motor Co., Inc. (1984), the plaintiff locked herself inside the trunk of defendant's car, intending to commit suicide; and then she could not get out after she changed her mind, and remained locked in the trunk for nine days. She sued for resulting psychological and physical injuries, alleging a design defect because the trunk would not open from the inside. In granting defendant's motion for summary judgment, the court noted that this was "not a case where a person inadvertently became trapped" in the trunk, and also that the design features and dimensions of the trunk made it "well near impossible that an adult intentionally would enter the trunk and close the lid."

Unforeseeable misuse was a complete bar to recovery in States v. R.D. Werner Co. (1990). Plaintiff was denied recovery for injuries from a ladder accident, where he alleged a defect in the aluminum rivets which secured the spreader bars connecting the front legs to the back legs of the ladder. He had positioned the front legs on a sidewalk, and the back legs on the unfinished surface of a parking lot some 6–9" below the level of the front legs. "This positioning was contrary to instructions for the proper use of the ladder which were affixed to the ladder itself," and was the sole proximate cause of the accident, the court held.

The jury verdict for the defendant in Bridges v. Chemrex Specialty Coatings, Inc. (1983), can be explained as a finding of no duty. There some neighborhood children apparently threw firecrackers into abandoned empty chemical drums, which exploded injuring the plaintiff. Defendant's label on the drums warned against exposure to heat or flame, and the drums were "discarded without resealing, contrary to the manufacturer's instructions." In finding for the defendant, the jury may well have found defendant discharged its duty by adequately warning of the danger.

Sidwell v. William Prym, Inc. (1986), shows the close relationship between duty and proximate cause. There the plaintiff was injured when a needle her mother was using to hem her dress was driven into her knee and shattered as she accidentally brushed against a coffee table. In denying recovery, the court described the injury as "a freak accident." It noted that "billions of such pins have been sold throughout the world without any complaints or problems." Perhaps the decisive feature of the case was the fact that the testimony of plaintiff's expert metallurgist as to defectiveness was excluded for lack of foundation, since the witness "had no knowledge whether the product in question had been designed with brittleness as a desirable attribute" and "had no expertise in the garment field."

In Landrine v. Mego Corp. (1983), the court found that the manufacturer of a balloon was not liable for the death of a child that choked on the balloon, which was incorporated into a toy "Bubble Yum" doll by a doll manufacturer. The doll was inflated by the balloon, and it simulated "the blow-ing of a bubble gum bubble". The child somehow managed to swallow the balloon that was used to inflate the doll. In granting summary judgment for defendant Perfect Products, the balloon manufacturer, the court said that "the record is barren of any evidence that Perfect knew or had any reason to know that its balloons would be inserted in 'Bubble Yum' dolls." Digestion of a balloon, the court said, "is a misuse of a product for which the guardian of children must be wary. Were it otherwise, anything capable of being swallowed would have to be kept from a child."

Garner v. Raven Industries, Inc. (1984) illustrates how questions of cause-in-fact and proximate cause can become intertwined. There plaintiff owned a helium-filled advertising balloon manufactured by defendant that broke away from its moorings, and it had to be pursued and shot down because its "automatic deflation device" failed to operate. After the balloon was shot down plaintiff pursued it on the ground, and was severely injured when he somehow became entangled in the balloon. Rejecting plaintiff's claim that the failure of the deflation device made the balloon defective and unreasonably dangerous, the court said that had the device worked properly the only difference would be that the "balloon would have descended at an earlier time"; and no evidence was presented which would substantiate plaintiff's claim "that had this occurred, he would not have been injured." Perhaps the plaintiff could have made a submissible case had he shown, for example, that the deflation device would have completely deflated the balloon so it would not have moved about on the ground, or that the balloon was subjected to movement by wind which would not have occurred had the device worked causing the balloon to descend sooner.

In Bigbee v. Pacific Tel. and Tel. Co. (1983), the court held that the plaintiff stated a cause of action against the companies "responsible for the design, location, installation and maintenance" of a telephone booth. Defendants had placed the booth, "which was difficult to exit, in a parking lot 15 feet from the side of a major thoroughfare and near a driveway." The plaintiff was allowed to sue for injuries sustained when an intoxicated driver left the thoroughfare and crashed into the booth. Plaintiff saw the driver coming and attempted to flee, but was unable to exit because "the door to the booth 'jammed and stuck, trapping' plaintiff inside." Under these circumstances, the court said, the risk could not "be said to be unforeseeable as a matter of law," particularly "where, as here, there is evidence that a booth at this same location had previously been struck."

## 3.  ALTERATION

A special problem of misuse concerns the alteration of a product. A substantial alteration that causes the accident may be unforeseeable barring recovery, unless the alteration should have been anticipated because of characteristics of the product that invite or encourage the change.

In Hollinger v. Wagner Min. Equip. Co. (1981), plaintiff sued for the death of a miner who was run down by a large earth-moving machine, called a scooptram. Plaintiff contended that the machine should have been equipped with an automatic warning device that would have alerted the deceased of the scooptram's approach.

Defendant contended that plaintiff's claim was barred because the machine had been substantially changed by the removal of a manual horn prior to the accident. Whether this constituted a "substantial" change so as to preclude liability, said the court, depended on whether the presence of the manual horn would have prevented the accident. The court said a jury could find that the horn might not have prevented the accident, both because the driver's vision was obscured so that he might not have seen the deceased in time to avoid the accident, and because the driver apparently assumed the deceased was aware of the approaching machine and therefore "would have had no reason to use the manual horn."

Similarly, in Witthauer v. Burkhart Roentgen, Inc. (1991), the court held that the distributor of a high-intensity surgical lamp had a duty to warn of the foreseeable dangers of dislodging the lamp's lower housing. The danger of heat burn from the lamp if the housing were displaced was not obvious.

Plaintiff in Anderson v. Dreis & Krump Mfg. Corp. (1987) contended that defendant's multi-purpose punch press was defectively designed because it lacked a point-of-operation guard to protect against the operator inserting his hands into the die area while the press was activated. Defendant asserted that the machine had been unforeseeably altered by the substitution of a single-button activation device for the two-button device with which the machine was originally furnished. The court held that "a jury could find it was reasonably foreseeable to Dreis that a purchaser of the press would choose an alternative method of activation given the press' myriad uses."

In some instances the product appears to invite alteration. Thus in Lopez v. Precision Papers, Inc. (1985), it was foreseeable that an overhead guard on a forklift truck would be removed because the truck was much more versatile without the guard. The plaintiff stated a cause or action based on defendant's furnishing a "nonwelded, easily removable" guard, and failing to provide a device that would indicate the weight of the load being lifted and failing to provide loading guidelines. In Nesselrode v. Executive Beechcraft, Inc. (1986), the right and left elevator trim tab actuators on a plane could be found defectively designed because of the risk of confusion, so that each actuator was installed on the wrong side of the plane resulting in a fatal crash. See also Airco, Inc. v. Simmons First Nat. Bank (1982) (danger of misconnection of selector valve on artificial breathing apparatus).

Where a defendant furnishes a defectively constructed product, it is foreseeable that the product
may be defectively modified in an attempt to correct the original defect. Guffie v. Erie Strayer Co.
(1965) (danger of spillage from conveyor belt sought
to be corrected by negligently constructed canopy
over work area).

In Manning v. Ashland Oil Co. (1983), the court
held the bulk supplier of a highly flammable lac-
quer thinner could reasonably rely on its knowl-
edgeable purchaser to properly label the product,
where the purchaser repackaged the thinner in
retail-size containers and improperly labeled the
product as suitable for removal of tar stains. In
Delk v. Holiday Inns, Inc. (1982), injuries caused by
the release of toxic fumes from defendant's carpet
and wall coverings, resulting from an arson fire,
were held unforeseeable. The fumes were released
under excessive temperature, the court said, and
not under ambient conditions. Presumably the
court would have reached the same result if the
fire had been accidentally caused, since it held the
defendant had no duty to design its product "to
perform under disaster conditions."

## 4.  DAMAGES

Sec. 435 of the Rest. 2d of Torts states:

(1) If the actor's conduct is a substantial factor
in bringing about harm to another, the fact that
the actor neither foresaw nor should have fore-

seen the extent of the harm or the manner in which it occurred does not prevent him from being liable.

(2) The actor's conduct may be held not to be a legal cause of harm to another where after the event and looking back from the harm to the actor's negligent conduct, it appears to the court highly extraordinary that it should have brought about the harm.

In Pope v. Rollins Protective Services Co. (1983), the court held it was foreseeable that the plaintiff would suffer mental anguish—for which she could recover substantial damages—as the result of being burglarized owing to defendant's defective burglar alarm.  In Prejean v. Great A. & P. Tea Co., Inc. (1984), the court held the plaintiff was entitled to recover for damages from vomiting, resulting in the tear of stomach tissue and loss of blood, on opening a package containing rotten, malodorous meat sold by the defendant.

In a 5–4 decision, the court in Jamieson v. Woodward & Lothrop (1957) held it unforeseeable that the plaintiff would suffer a detached retina when defendant's rubber exerciser rope slipped off her feet and contracted, hitting her in the eye while she was using the rope as directed.  The court held that the "reasonably foreseeable injury from a mishap with this rope was not great—a cut lip, bloody nose, or black eye, at the most."  It also said the article was "a simple thing of universally known characteristics," whose danger was "not latent but obvious." The dissent thought that the extent of the danger was not so obvious as to preclude a claim for defective design and warning, and that liability for damages "turns upon the foreseeability of any harm ... not upon the foreseeability of the exact nature and extent of the injury which does in fact ensue."

In Feldman v. Lederle Laboratories (1992) plaintiff's teeth were discolored by tetracycline staining. Part of the injury occurred before, and part after, the defendant's duty to warn arose. The court found that plaintiff's injury was "incremental" rather than indivisible, and that plaintiff's expert could make a "reasonable estimate" as to the time and extent of the injury.

## C. PLAINTIFF MISCONDUCT, AND COMPARATIVE FAULT

### 1. THE TYPES OF MISCONDUCT

The three major types of plaintiff misconduct that can bar or limit the plaintiff's right of recovery are contributory negligence, assumption of the risk, and misuse including alteration of the product. Contributory negligence is the failure of the plaintiff to take reasonable care for his own safety. Assumption of the risk is a knowing and voluntary confrontation of an appreciated risk. Misuse is the use of a product in a foreseeable or unforeseeable manner.

Contributory negligence and assumption of the risk are usually treated as defenses, with the burden of proof on the defendant. Contributory negligence is determined by a reasonable-person standard, while assumption of the risk is based on the subjective knowledge of what the plaintiff actually knew. As noted in the previous section, there is a division of authority as to whether proof of misuse is treated as a defense, or whether its disproof is treated as part of plaintiff's case-in-chief.

The danger is frequently, although not always, obvious when the defense of assumption of the risk is raised. The danger can also be latent but discovered by the plaintiff. Where the danger is obvious, obviousness should not be a separate basis for denying recovery but should go only to the defense of assumption of the risk, as the court recognized in Gann v. International Harvester Co. of Canada, Ltd. (1986). An obvious warning, however, may bar recovery not merely because of its obviousness, but because of its adequacy both in content and method of communication.

A plaintiff may be aware of one risk without appreciating another. In Hobbs v. Armco, Inc. (1982), the plaintiff had knowledge of the general danger of "pipes sliding off the V-door ramp"; but he allegedly had no specific knowledge that the "hook of the air hoist line, which secured the pipe, had come loose" when he was injured by such an unsecured pipe falling from the ramp. The evidence presented a factual issue, precluding a finding of assumption of the risk as a matter of law.

There is no bright line between the types of plaintiff misconduct, and the same conduct "can often be the basis for any one of the three defenses." Young v. Up–Right Scaffolds, Inc. (1980). How the conduct is characterized can make a significant difference in the outcome of a case, however. In Lippard v. Houdaille Indus., Inc. (1986), the court held that while contributory negligence did not apply to a strict products liability suit in that state, the defendant could nevertheless "sometimes make use of the plaintiff's alleged carelessness in support of arguments that the product is not unreasonably dangerous, or that the alleged defects in a product did not cause the injury." Arguments based on such evidence, the court said, "are traversing claims not appropriate for instruction."

"There is a sharp split of authority amongst courts that have considered the admissibility of safety-belt evidence," the court said in Swajian v. General Motors Corp. (1989). The court there aligned itself "with the majority of jurisdictions in holding that a plaintiff owes no duty to anticipate a defendant's negligence and to minimize damages by buckling up *before* the tortious impact occurs." Some states by statute prohibit the introduction of evidence of failure to wear a seat belt, while others "limit the amount of reduction in the award, such as Michigan and Iowa (5%), Louisiana (2%), and

Missouri (1%)". LaHue v. General Motors Corp. (1989).

Assumption of the risk may be an inappropriate defense for workplace injuries, owing to workplace pressures and the worker's need to retain the job which makes exposure to known dangers reasonable or not voluntary. Johansen v. Makita USA, Inc. (1992). There are other instances when exposure to a known danger may be reasonable, as for example in Devaney v. Sarno (1973), where plaintiff continued to drive his car while awaiting replacement parts for a defective seat belt. Such continued use could be found reasonable, since plaintiff needed the automobile and was not told by the dealer that he should not operate it.

In the section below on comparative fault, it will be seen that mere inadvertence or failure to discover a danger is sometimes not a defense and does not reduce damages in strict liability or negligence under comparative fault principles. In the few jurisdictions that retain the defense of contributory negligence as a complete bar to recovery in negligence, it is possible that a similar exception will be made.

Conversely, the plaintiff's status may bar recovery as a matter of law. Some courts have held that the so-called "fireman's rule" bars recovery by a professional rescuer for injuries caused by the negligence of one creating the need for the rescue. There is a division of authority "as to the rule's application in a products liability or strict liability

context." Mahoney v. Carus Chem. Co., Inc.
(1986). The courts that apply the rule to bar
recovery in products liability do so on the grounds
that the professional rescuer assumes the risk of
those hazards which are known or can reasonably
be anticipated at the site of the rescue, since he is
hired to confront just such risks. The rule does
not bar recovery for unusual or unanticipated
risks, and many courts hold that it does not bar
recovery for injury from a hazard created by wilful
or wanton misconduct. The lay rescuer is not
barred, however, Guarino v. Mine Safety Appliance
Co. (1969). Many courts apply comparative fault
principles to the negligent lay rescuer, but in Ouel-
lette v. Carde (1992) the court said such a rescuer's
recovery would be reduced "only if a defendant
establishes that the rescuer's actions were rash or
reckless."

## 2. THE EFFECT OF PLAINTIFF MISCON-DUCT IN STRICT LIABILITY (WITH-OUT COMPARATIVE FAULT)

Some courts hold that contributory negligence is
no defense in a strict products liability action, but
that assumption of the risk is a defense. Remy v.
Michael D's Carpet Outlets (1990). This position is
advocated in comment *n* of the Rest. 2d of Torts,
§ 402A:

> *n. Contributory negligence.* Since the liabili-
> ty with which this Section deals is not based

upon negligence of the seller, but is strict liability, the rule applied to strict liability cases (see § 524) applies.  Contributory negligence of the plaintiff is not a defense when such negligence consists merely in a failure to discover the defect in the product, or to guard against the possibility of its existence.  On the other hand the form of contributory negligence which consists in voluntarily and unreasonably proceeding to encounter a known danger, and commonly passes under the name of assumption of risk, is a defense under this Section as in other cases of strict liability.  If the user or consumer discovers the defect and is aware of the danger, and nevertheless proceeds unreasonably to make use of the product and is injured by it, he is barred from recovery.

Unforeseeable misuse of a product, whether by the plaintiff or another, is a bar to recovery in strict liability for injuries proximately caused by such misuse.  In order to recover from a product manufacturer, the plaintiff must prove that the product was defective and the proximate cause of his injury.  A product is defective when it is unreasonably dangerous for normal or foreseeable use.  Where a bottle of cola was subjected to a "combination of agitation, heat and a severe impact," the jury was justified in finding that the explosion of the bottle was not caused by a product defect.  Tyler v. Natchitoches Coca–Cola Bottling Co. (1986).

## 3. COMPARATIVE FAULT

### a. Kinds of Comparison

Comparative fault has been widely adopted, either by statute or by judicial decision. The court in McIntyre v. Balentine (1992) stated that as of the date of that decision thirty-four states had adopted comparative fault by statute, and twelve states (including the court in that decision) had adopted it by judicial decision.

There are three principal patterns of comparison: the plaintiff can recover if 1) her fault is less than that of the defendant, 2) if it is not more than that of the defendant, or 3) if the defendant is at fault in any degree. The first two methods are called modified or partial comparative fault, whereby the plaintiff is barred entirely if his fault 1) equals, or 2) exceeds that of the defendant. One of these two methods has usually been chosen by legislative adoption. The third method, called pure comparative fault, is preferred by commentators and is the method usually chosen by judicial adoption.

If the plaintiff is permitted to recover, her recovery will be proportionately reduced by the percentage of fault, if any, attributable to herself. Thus, a plaintiff found 30% at fault can recover 70% of her damages.

Where there is more than one defendant, the general rule is to retain joint and several liability in comparative fault. So, in the comparative fault case of Rozevink v. Faris (1983) (nonproducts case, motorcycle-car collision), where the plaintiff was found free of fault and the defendants 17% and 83% at fault, respectively, the 17%-at-fault defendant was held liable for the entire damages. The reasons for retaining joint liability in comparative fault, even where the plaintiff is also at fault, are stated in Coney v. J.L.G. Indus., Inc. (1983):

(1) The feasibility of apportioning fault on a comparative basis does not render an indivisible injury "divisible" for purposes of the joint and several liability rule. A concurrent tortfeasor is liable for the whole of an indivisible injury when his negligence is a proximate cause of that damage. In many instances, the negligence of each concurrent tortfeasor may be sufficient by itself to cause the entire loss. The mere fact that it may be possible to assign some percentage figure to the relative culpability of one negligent defendant as compared to another does not in any way suggest that each defendant's negligence is not a proximate cause of the entire indivisible injury.

(2) In those instances where the plaintiff is not guilty of negligence, he would be forced to bear a portion of the loss should one of the tortfeasors prove financially unable to satisfy his share of the damages.

(3) Even in cases where a plaintiff is partially at fault, his culpability is not equivalent to that of a defendant. The plaintiff's negligence relates

only to a lack of due care for his own safety while the defendant's negligence relates to a lack of due care for the safety of others; the latter is tortious, but the former is not.

(4) Elimination of joint and several liability would work a serious and unwarranted deleterious effect on the ability of an injured plaintiff to obtain adequate compensation for his injuries.

Some jurisdictions have abolished joint and several liability either in its entirety, or in certain circumstances as for example where defendant's fault is less than that of the plaintiff or for certain types of damages such as recovery for pain and suffering. The court in Vannoy v. Uniroyal Tire Co. (1985) held that the jury in either a negligence or a strict liability action must apportion damages among all possible defendants regardless of whether they are parties to the suit and regardless of whether it is "possible to establish liability for various reasons including immunity, settlement, failure to join as a party, unknown identity, statute of limitations, or numerous other possible causes." The Unif. Comparat. Fault Act § 2(d), 12 U.L.A. 41 (1986 Supp.), adopts a compromise approach. It retains joint liability; but, where one defendant is unable to pay in contribution, the uncollectible portion attributable to that defendant is apportioned between the plaintiff and any solvent defendant or defendants according to their respective degrees of fault.

A different type of problem arises where there are multiple defendants, in a jurisdiction that has adopted modified or partial comparative fault. Regardless of whether the defendants in such a jurisdiction can be held liable either jointly or severally, the plaintiff will be barred entirely if his comparative fault exceeds a certain amount (49% in some jurisdictions, 50% in others). In making the fault comparison, there is a division of authority as to whether the plaintiff's fault is compared with each defendant separately, or with all defendants together. Erickson v. Whirlpool Corp. (1990). If the comparison is made with all defendants, it is apparent that a defendant less at fault than the plaintiff may nevertheless be held liable. Where comparison is made with each defendant, a defendant less at fault than the plaintiff may, however, be liable for contribution to another defendant if the jurisdiction imposes joint liability and contribution is available against a tortfeasor who is not liable to the plaintiff by reason of comparative fault immunity.

Where the plaintiff can be barred from recovery entirely if his fault exceeds a certain percentage, it is not uncommon for the court to adopt a rule that the jury must be instructed as to the effect of its verdict on recovery. See, e.g., Sheldon v. Unit Rig & Equipment Co. (1986). The purpose of this rule is apparently to permit the jury to adjust its determination of percentages of fault depending on whether or not it wishes the plaintiff to be barred entirely.

Comparative fault is widely applied to unreasonable assumption of the risk, Watson v. Navistar Int'l Transp. Corp. (1992). Some courts still retain assumption of the risk as a complete bar, however, even after the adoption of comparative fault. Bonds v. Snapper Power Equip. Co. (1991) If a court applies the doctrine of assumption of risk to describe a situation where no duty is owed, either because there is no negligence on the part of the defendant or the defendant is immune, see Mahoney v. Carus Chem. Co., Inc. (1986) (fireman's rule), then presumably such assumption of the risk would continue to be a complete bar even when comparative fault is adopted. Conversely, if the rule is that certain conduct—such as plaintiff's failure to wear a seat belt or plaintiff's awareness of danger in the workplace—is deemed irrelevant to contributory negligence or assumption of the risk, this rule may survive the adoption of comparative fault.

As will be seen in the next section, some courts apply comparative fault to conduct based on plaintiff misuse of the product. This makes sense where the misuse is foreseeable and resembles contributory negligence. Where the misuse is unforeseeable, however, or where it establishes the absence of a defect or of proximate cause, there should be no comparison made since no duty is owed.

In Champagne v. Raybestos–Manhattan (1989), an asbestos case, the court upheld a 75% reduction of the plaintiff's recovery because of his smoking. Plaintiff's deceased was repeatedly warned by doctors to stop smoking after his lung problem was discovered. There was evidence "that the incidence of cancer in smokers exposed to asbestos is from ten to sixty times more than the incidence of cancer in nonsmokers exposed to asbestos." But in Martin v. Owens–Corning Fiberglas Corp. (1987) the court held that evidence of plaintiff's smoking could not be used to reduce the plaintiff's recovery for asbestosis and related diseases, where the defendant failed to introduce sufficient proof to support apportionment of damages.

Some courts compare relative fault, others relative causation, and still others a combination of these factors in determining comparative fault or comparative responsibility. See Sandford v. Chevrolet Division of General Motors (1982). Comparative fault or causation can be used to reduce damages in crashworthiness cases, where defendant's conduct does not cause the accident but merely increases the injuries, Keltner v. Ford Motor Co. (1984). It can be used in cases where plaintiff fails to avoid the consequences of defendant's tortious conduct, McDonald v. Federal Labs., Inc. (1984) (defective mace, 15% damage reduction for plaintiff's failure to remove mace-soaked clothes); and where plaintiff's and defendant's conduct is a continuing contribution to the injury, Fulgium v. Armstrong World Indus., Inc. (1986) (asbestos exposure, recovery reduced by amount of injury attributable to plaintiff's smoking). The apportionment must be based on reasonable evidence, however, and not on "speculation and conjecture." *Martin v. Owens–Corning Fiberglas*, supra. A comparative-causation approach may help solve conceptual difficulties where the comparison is between a negligent plaintiff and a strictly liable defendant, as discussed in the next section.

### b. In Strict Liability

Some states by statute apply comparative fault to strict liability actions. Austin v. Raybestos–Manhattan, Inc. (1984). In others, the statute may be limited to negligence actions—in which event the court may, Day v. General Motors Corp. (1984), or may not, Young's Machine Co. v. Long (1984), Lippard v. Houdaille Indus., Inc. (1986), extend comparative fault to strict liability by judicial decision. Some courts have adopted comparative fault in strict liability by judicial decision without any applicable statute, while others have refused to do so. Staymates v. ITT Holub Indus. (1987). Comparative fault has been adopted in strict tort liability in admiralty, Lewis v. Timco, Inc. (1983), and a majority of jurisdictions that have considered the issue have extended comparative fault to warranty suits, Kennedy v. City of Sawyer (1980). Where there is a comparative fault statute that is construed to apply only to negligence actions, and the court extends comparative fault to strict liability by judicial decision, the judicial extension may not parallel the statutory basis of liability. For example, a statute may use partial comparative fault for negligence actions, and the court may extend the doctrine to strict liability on a pure comparative-fault basis. Sheldon v. Unit Rig & Equipment Co. (1986).

The courts also differ as to whether or not plaintiff's contributory negligence should be used to reduce recovery or should simply be disregarded in strict liability, and in addressing this issue they differ regarding the type of contributory negligence that should or should not be compared. Some courts in applying a comparative fault statute, Austin v. Raybestos–Manhattan (1984), or by judicial extension of such a statute, Mauch v. Manufacturers Sales & Serv., Inc. (1984), hold that contributory negligence should not be compared in strict liability—thus carrying forward the pre-comparative fault rule regarding contributory negligence in strict liability. Others state that contributory negligence should be compared—except when it consists of mere failure to discover, Keen v. Ashot Ashkelon, Ltd. (1988), or "mere carelessness or inadvertence," Johansen v. Makita USA, Inc. (1992), which is not used to reduce recovery. Still others hold that even mere momentary forgetfulness, Keller v. Vermeer Mfg. Co. (1984), or inadvertence, Winston v. International Harvester Corp. (1986), should be compared along with any other type of contributory negligence. Kentucky adopted comparative fault by judicial rule, Hilen v. Hays (1984). The legislature initially prohibited, see Reda Pump Co. v. Finck (1986), and then applied, this rule in products suits, Ky.Rev.Stats. 411.182 (1992).

Following the pre-comparative fault rule occasionally applied, some courts hold that the comparative fault doctrine is inapplicable to workplace injuries in strict liability, whether plaintiff's conduct consists of mere inadvertence, Robertson v. Superior PMI, Inc. (1986), or assumption of the risk, Bell v. Jet Wheel Blast (1985). The court in Green v. Sterling Extruder Corp. (1984), extended this holding to a suit in negligence, saying:

> The practicalities of the workaday world are such that in the vast majority of cases, the employee works "as is" or he is without a job.... It would be anomalous to hold that defendant has a duty to install safety devices but that a breach of that duty results in no liability for the very injury the duty was meant to protect against.

Some courts say that plaintiff misuse is also to be compared in strict liability. Simpson v. General Motors Corp. (1985). Thus in Duncan v. Cessna Aircraft Co. (1984), the court held that comparative causation should be applied in strict liability whether the plaintiff's conduct "is characterized as assumption of risk, misuse, or failure to mitigate or avoid damages." The court in Mauch v. Manufacturers Sales & Serv., Inc. (1984), went so far as to hold that comparative principles apply when the plaintiff's "unforeseeable misuse" of the product is a "concurring proximate cause" of the injury. Presumably unforeseeable misuse would bar recovery in comparative fault, however, when such misuse, rather than a defect, was the proximate cause of the injury.  See Tyler v. Natchitoches Coca–Cola Bottling Co. (1986) (bottle explosion caused by agitation and heat combined with a severe impact).

## D.  SUBSEQUENT REMEDIAL MEASURES

Fed. R. Evid. 407 provides:

When, after an event, measures are taken which, if taken previously, would have made the event less likely to occur, evidence of the subsequent measures is not admissible to prove negligence or culpable conduct in connection with the event.  This rule does not require the exclusion of evidence of subsequent measures when offered for another purpose, such as proving ownership, control, or feasibility of precautionary measures, if controverted, or impeachment.

A similar provision exists in many state laws.

The rule is generally held to exclude evidence of remedial measures only if taken by the defendant after the plaintiff's injury, and it does not exclude evidence of such measures taken before the injury. Huffman v. Caterpillar Tractor Co. (1990).  The rationale for admitting evidence of pre-accident remedial measures presumably is that the defendant is not likely to be discouraged from taking such measures if he is unaware of the plaintiff's potential claim against him. If that be the case, then such evidence should be admissible only when the defendant is unaware of any potential claim, not just when he is unaware of the plaintiff's claim.

Nor does the rule exclude evidence of remedial measures taken by one other than the defendant. Blaw–Knox Construc. Equip. Co. v. Morris (1991). But in Bingham v. Marshall & Huschart (1992) the court excluded evidence of third-party remedial measures under the state's counterpart of Fed. R. Evid. 403 (probative value of evidence was substantially outweighed "by the danger of unfair prejudice, confusion of the issues, or misleading of the jury"). Similarly, evidence of remedial measures taken by a third party may be excluded on grounds of remoteness. Grenada Steel Indus., Inc. v. Alabama Oxygen Co., Inc. (1983). Presumably the *Bingham* and *Grenada* rationales for excluding evidence of remedial measures could be used whether the measures were taken by the defendant or by a third party.

The rule also does not exclude evidence of remedial measures taken by a defendant after the plaintiff's accident when those measures are involuntarily undertaken, as for example by a government-mandated recall. Herndon v. Seven Bar Flying Service, Inc. (1983). The rationale for the exclusionary rule is that the admission of such evidence will discourage the defendant from taking remedial measures, but that rationale does not apply when the measures are undertaken involuntarily.  Millette v. Radosta (1980).

The rule does not apply unless the evidence concerns conduct that can fairly be described as a remedial measure.  The defendant in Rocky Mountain Helicopters, Inc. v. Bell Helicopters Textron (1986) undertook a study of the performance characteristics of the trunnions on its helicopters, after plaintiff's helicopter crashed allegedly due to fatigue failure of a trunnion, and then later the defendant redesigned its trunnions as a result of the study.  Although evidence of the redesign was excluded by R. 407, evidence of the study was admitted because the court found it was not a subsequent remedial measure.  Similarly, in Prentiss & Carlisle Company, Inc. v. Koehring–Waterous Div. of Timberjack, Inc. (1992) a report of defendant's post-accident investigation was admitted where the remedial recommendations were excised from the report.

The rule excludes evidence only "when offered to prove negligence or culpable conduct," and a number of courts have held that the rule does not apply to a strict liability suit since fault is not in issue in such a case.  Ault v. International Harvester (1974).  Other courts state that the exclusionary policy of the rule applies whether the defendant is sued in negligence or strict liability, since by "excluding this evidence, defendants are encouraged to make such improvements.  From a defendant's point of view, it is the fact that the evidence may be used against him which will inhibit subsequent repairs or improvement. It makes no difference to the defendant on what theory the evidence is admitted (negligence or strict liability) because his inclination to make subsequent improvements will be similarly inhibited." Hallmark v. Allied Products Corp. (1982).

Part of the rationale in *Ault,* supra, for admitting evidence of subsequent remedial measures is that the admission of such evidence will not discourage the defendant from taking remedial measures where it "manufactures tens of thousands of units of goods; it is manifestly unrealistic to suggest that such a producer will forego making improvements in its product, and risk innumerable additional lawsuits and the attendant adverse effect upon its public image," simply because the evidence of improvements might be admitted in a lawsuit.

The court in D.L. by Friederichs v. Huebner (1983) declined to draw a distinction between defendants based on size, where the defendant contended that it was not a "mass manufacturer" and therefore that the *Ault* rationale for admitting evidence of remedial measures was inapplicable. The record contained no evidence about "Huebner Implements' 'size' compared with other manufacturers," nor did Huebner suggest any guidelines or any "reasonable basis on which a court might fashion an administrable rule distinguishing between manufacturers or sellers based on their relative sizes." Finally, the justification for the doctrine of strict products liability "is applicable to both large and small manufacturers" and the court had not previously distinguished between classes of manufacturers in imposing strict liability, and "we can find no sound reasons for our doing so in this case."

Evidence of subsequent remedial measures may be admitted, even in a negligence case, if offered for some purpose other than that of showing negligence or culpable conduct. Herndon v. Seven Bar Flying Service, Inc. (1983). It is a well-accepted rule that evidence which is inadmissible for one purpose may nevertheless be admissible for another purpose, with a limiting instruction as to the purpose for which the evidence is admitted.

R. 407 states that evidence of subsequent remedial measures is admissible when offered to prove "feasibility of precautionary measures, if controverted, or impeachment." The feasibility of providing a safer design or warning is often a principal issue in products litigation, but a variety of positions have developed on the issue for purposes of determining the admissibility of evidence under R. 407. The difficulty is in determining when the defendant has "controverted" feasibility. In Gauthier v. AMF, Inc. (1986), the court held that defendant did not controvert feasibility when it "admitted that the engineering knowledge was available in 1972 to install deadman controls and the cost was not prohibitive," but it refused to agree to a stipulation that the safety devices were "feasible" for fear the jury "would interpret the word too broadly." It then asserted "that the safety problem was not great enough to warrant the trade-off of consumer frustration, increased complexity of the product, and risk of consumer efforts to disconnect the safety device." The defendant was thus controverting the practicality of the change, which the court considered to be different from feasibility.

Similarly, in Probus v. K–Mart, Inc. (1986), the court held that the defendant did not controvert the feasibility of a change in the design of a plastic tip on an aluminum ladder, where it did not contend "that the material used in the end cap was either the best material available or that the use of another material would not have been feasible." Defendant rather contended that the cap "was appropriate for its application" and was fractured "by a type of impact not arising out of normal usage." In Fish v. Georgia–Pacific Corp. (1985), the appellate court held that the trial court erred in admitting evidence of a 1983 warning by the plaintiff, offered to prove the feasibility of a warning in 1977 of the dangers of formaldehyde emissions from defendant's particleboard. The defendant "was willing to admit the feasibility of providing a warning in 1977," but "simply contended that it did not have a legal duty to do so."

Recognizing the difficulty of determining when the issue of feasibility is controverted, the court in

Herndon v. Seven Bar Flying Service, Inc. (1983) indicated that feasibility should be deemed controverted unless the defendant "is prepared to make an unequivocal admission of feasibility" and "concedes that at the time of the accident it would have been possible to make a safer product." This was a sensible rule, the court said, "even where the feasibility of remedial measures is as apparent as in our case." Similarly, in Simmons v. Monarch Machine Tool Co., Inc. (1992) the court held that evidence of defendant's post-accident design improvement was admissible in the discretion of the trial court "to prove the practical possibility of making a safety improvement," and the evidence was not rendered inadmissible "simply because of a general concession of feasibility" by the defendant.

It is possible that a subsequent remedial measure by the defendant will be treated as an admission, and admitted into evidence on that basis. The U.S. Supreme Court in Columbia & P.S.R. Co. v. Hawthorne (1892) held that "the taking of such precautions against the future is not to be construed as an admission of responsibility for the past." Since evidence of admissions is favored by the courts, however, the *Hawthorne* rule may not be good law today.

A recall letter by the defendant may be admitted as evidence of an admission. In re Multi–Piece Rims Products Liability Litigation (1982). Contra, Vockie v. General Motors Corp. (1975). Evidence of a recall by the defendant was admitted in Hessen v. Jaguar Cars, Inc. (1990).

In General Motors Corp. v. Johnston (1992) a $7.5 million wrongful death judgment was entered based in part on evidence of defendant's "silent" or "unpublished" recall campaign. A defective memory chip caused the pickup truck of plaintiff's deceased to stall, resulting in the deceased's death. Defendant would replace the chip whenever a customer made a complaint, without explaining the problem to the customer. The evidence indicated that defendant saved approximately $42 million by not engaging in a full-scale campaign.

As discussed in the chapter on warnings, a defendant may have a post-sale or continuing duty to warn. In this situation, evidence of post-accident remedial measures may be admissible on the rationale that since the defendant is legally obliged to make the changes, admission of the evidence will not discourage him from doing so. See Herndon v. Seven Bar Flying Service, Inc. (1983) (Rule 407 inapplicable to exclude evidence of defendant's post-sale directives required by FAA).

Some states have "state-of-the-art" statutes providing that the scientific and technological knowledge available when a product is first sold for consumer use controls in deciding if the product is defective. The court in Ragsdale v. K–Mart Corp. (1984) said that such a statute did not prevent the admission of evidence of subsequent remedial measures by the defendant. The court in Witherspoon

v. Ciba–Geigy Corp. (1986), on the other hand, indicated that a state-of-the-art statute would prevent the admission of evidence of subsequent warnings by the defendant. As indicated below in the section on state of the art, some courts rely on Rule 407 as a basis for using the date of trial as the time for determining state of the art.

## E.  MISCELLANEOUS PROBLEMS OF PROOF

### 1.  HISTORY OF UNSAFE AND SAFE USE

Evidence of unsafe use and of prior accidents with similar products is admissible for a variety of purposes, including proof of notice of the alleged defect by the defendant, the magnitude of the danger, the foreseeability of user conduct, the defendant's ability to correct the defect, and causation. Tacke v. Vermeer Mfg. Co. (1986); Rhodes v. Michelin Tire Corp. (1982). Such evidence is admissible in the discretion of the trial judge on a finding of sufficient similarity of conditions, provided the evidence is not too technical or remote in time, and does not trigger extensive inquiry into collateral matters. In *Rhodes* the court properly exercised its discretion in admitting evidence of a tearing condition that developed in 200 flaps of defendant's tires that were used in plaintiff's truck fleet, where plaintiff alleged that a similar tear caused the accident in litigation. In *Tacke* the trial court abused its discretion in excluding evidence of similar accidents about which the plaintiff learned from defendant's answers to interrogatories.

In Rexrode v. American Laundry Press Co. (1982), the court indicated that the preferable way for determining the admissibility of other-accident evidence is to hold a hearing on relevancy outside the jury's presence. The trial court there did not abuse its discretion, however, in permitting plaintiff's counsel to cross-examine defendant's expert witnesses regarding similar accidents which they had investigated. The evidence was relevant to determine notice, the existence of a defect, or to refute defense testimony that the product was designed without safety hazards.

The court in Johnson v. Colt Industries Operating Corp. (1986) held it error to admit a judicial opinion from another lawsuit to establish defendant's notice of a similar accident, in a case involving the alleged defective design of defendant's colt .22 revolver. Such evidence should be admitted only when similar-accident evidence can be obtained from no other source, and then only with detailed limiting instructions to avoid the jury's giving such evidence too much weight. The admission of the evidence was harmless error, however, in view of the strongly probative evidence of defectiveness introduced in plaintiff's case-in-chief.

Although the cases are divided, the "modern trend" is to admit evidence of the non-occurrence of prior accidents to show lack of product defectiveness, and lack of defendant's knowledge of the danger in a negligence case.   Minichello v. United States Indus., Inc. (1985).

In Jones v. Pak–Mor Mfg. Co. (1985), the court overruled its per-se rule that excluded evidence of safe history in every case, holding that there "is little logic in the proposition that the trial court may admit evidence of other accidents but may never admit evidence of their absence."   It recognized, however, that "defendant's 'lack of notice' of injury does not establish the fact that no injuries had occurred," that it is "harder to prove that something did not happen than to prove that it did happen," and that if "a product is very widely distributed, it will be almost impossible to rebut such a contention [of no prior accidents] when the real issue is simply whether, among millions of users, a few each year may have used the product in a way which produced serious injuries."   The court should weigh these considerations in determining whether the probative value of the evidence is substantially outweighed by the danger of prejudice, confusion, and waste of time.   The evidence should not be admitted unless "the witness was in such a position or has such sources of knowledge that if the event had occurred, he would have seen it or would have known about it."   Where the nature of the danger is "plain", such as an "open hole in a sidewalk", evidence of the lack of prior accidents "creates a considerable risk of misleading the jury," since all it shows is that "the plaintiff was the first to fall in the hole."

In a case of food poisoning allegedly caused by defendant's salad bar, evidence of lack of complaints on the same day plaintiff became ill was held inadmissible in Goins v. Wendy's Int'l, Inc. (1991). There were 117 salads served that day, and the names of the consumers were unknown, as were the specific items they ate and when they ate.

## 2.  SPOLIATION

Spoliation occurs when a person wilfully or negligently disposes of product evidence vital to a litigant's case. The person who disposes of the evidence may be held liable to the litigant for the damages she likely could have recovered but for the disposal. The disposer may be the product supplier, or another owing a duty to preserve the evidence. If the disposal makes it impossible to show that the product was defective, presumably the product's defectiveness can be implied. Conversely, spoliation by the plaintiff may bar a claim against the defendant.

In Wilson v. Beloit Corp. (1989) the court held that an employer could be liable in tort to an employee for disposing of machine parts vital to the employee's product claim against the machine manufacturer, provided the employee could show that the employer owed the employee a duty to preserve the parts. A similar claim was upheld against the police in Ober v. City of Plantation (1988) for disposing of a helmet the plaintiff was wearing in a motorcycle accident. The court in Murray v. Farmers Ins. Co. (1990) said that had the evidence not otherwise established the product's nondefectiveness, the plaintiff's attorney could be liable for failing to preserve the wrecked remains of plaintiff's automobile.

## 3.   EXPERT TESTIMONY

Expert testimony may be essential in a products liability lawsuit to establish a prima facie case of defectiveness, causation, damages, and other issues in the suit. Expert testimony is generally admissible if it will aid the fact finder in its determination of an issue in the suit. An expert may not be permitted to testify, however, if the subject matter of her testimony concerns a matter of common knowledge, and of course the expert cannot testify if she lacks the requisite qualifications of an expert in the field.

In Dambacher by Dambacher v. Mallis (1984), plaintiffs recovered against the defendant distributor, Sears, Roebuck & Co., for failure to warn of the danger of mixing radial and non-radial tires on an automobile. The appellate court upheld the trial court's determination that plaintiffs' experts were qualified to testify as to the need for such a warning:

While it is true that neither of these experts had extensive academic experience or had conducted rigidly controlled experiments concerning the effects of mixed tire type fitment on automobile handling, both claimed to have driven vehicles with such mixed fitment and to be aware of the adverse handling characteristics of such vehicles, and, as well, claimed familiarity with some of the literature and regulations in the field. The qualifications of an expert and the competency of his testimony, to a considerable extent, are matters within the discretion of the court below.

As to the need for such expert testimony, the court said:

In the present case both of the Dambachers' expert witnesses were shown to have knowledge of relevant areas of technology beyond that of laymen. Both experts were also cognizant of the general public's lack of knowledge concerning the dangers of mixing radial and non-radial tires on the same axle of a vehicle.

Experts may be lay persons, in the sense of lacking academic credentials, provided they have acquired specialized knowledge through experience with the product. Academic experts may be qualified to testify regarding physical, chemical or other principles or properties of a product without having designed or worked extensively with the particular product in issue, as long as such principles or properties are relevant to the issues in litigation and will aid the fact finder in resolving those issues.

An expert need not be familiar with all the aspects of the subject matter of his testimony, in order to be qualified. In Ellis v. K–Lan Co. (1983), an expert was permitted to testify regarding the need for a child-proof container cap on an acid-based drain declogger and the inadequacy of the warning on the container, although the expert was unfamiliar with the definition of a child-proof cap contained in a federal act on the subject. His lack of familiarity with the statutory definition "affects his credibility, not his qualifications to testify."

An expert may be permitted to testify on an ultimate fact in issue. In Karns v. Emerson Elec. Co. (1987), plaintiff's expert was permitted to testify that defendant's brush-cutting device was "unreasonably dangerous beyond the expectation of the average consumer" and that defendant "acted recklessly" in producing and distributing the product:

Fed. R. Evid. 704(a) provides that an expert's opinion testimony "is not objectionable because it embraces an ultimate issue to be decided by the trier of fact." Opinions embracing legal standards may, however, be excluded for other reasons, such as the likelihood of jury confusion, the danger of unfair prejudice, or the inability of such evidence to assist the trier of fact.... These are matters committed to the trial court's discretion, and we review a decision admitting or excluding such testimony only for abuse of that discretion.

Under Fed. R. Evid. 703 an expert may rely on facts or data that "need not be admissible in evidence," in forming an opinion or inference, as long as the evidence is "of a type reasonably relied upon by experts in the particular field." The comment to this Rule indicates that such evidence includes "statements by patients and relatives, reports and opinions from nurses, technicians and other doctors, hospital records, and x rays." It also includes "public opinion poll evidence." In Rubanick v. Witco Chemical Corp. (1991) the court cautioned against independent judicial review of the facts on which an expert bases his opinion. The trial court there improperly "substituted its own assessment of the studies for that of an acknowledged expert." The proper inquiry, the court said, was whether comparable experts in the field would reasonably rely on the data and information.

The U.S. Supreme Court in Daubert v. Merrill Dow Pharmaceuticals, Inc. (1993) rejected the "general acceptance" test of Frye v. U.S. (1923). It adopted a flexible, "reliable basis" test for admissibility of expert testimony.

There are a number of difficulties encountered in using expert testimony based on epidemiological studies as proof of product causation. The size of the sample, and the length and duration of exposure are variable factors, and it is difficult to estimate the effect of other causes that may intervene. Courts differ regarding the degree of probability required before such evidence is admissible.

Compare Brock v. Merrell Dow Pharmaceuticals, Inc. (1989) (Bendectin, very high probability required) with DeLuca v. Merrell Dow Pharmaceuticals, Inc. (1990) (same product, reasonableness standard used). Epidemiological evidence is more likely to be sufficient to establish causation when accompanied by other, case-specific evidence. Landrigan v. Celotex Corp. (1992).

## 4. STATE OF THE ART AND INDUSTRY CUSTOM

The definitions and role of state of the art and industry custom evidence were discussed in Chapter I, and in this Chapter in the section on subsequent remedial measures. As noted in those sections, courts have difficulty in distinguishing between state of the art and industry custom, and a number of courts permit evidence of industry custom to show state of the art. See Annot., 47 ALR 4th 621 (1986).

State of the art is usually defined as the scientific or technological knowledge available or existing when a product is marketed. In theory, at least, such knowledge—or, more accurately, such knowability—need not be the same as, or even reflect, what people actually know or actually are doing, or even what they should know or should be doing at a particular time or place. Nor need such knowability necessarily reflect practicality, in terms of economic costs or social utility. See American

Text. Mfrs. Inst., Inc. v. Donovan (1981) (feasibility under OSHA defined in terms of capability, in which cost is not determinative). Thus it is feasible to make a tank-like car that is virtually accident-proof, but such a car may be unacceptably expensive and not very useful for speedy travel.

Some courts admit evidence of knowledge or capability as of the date of trial to determine state of the art. Dart v. Wiebe Mfg., Inc. (1985). Accord, In re Asbestos Cases (1987); Habecker v. Clark Equip. Co. (1991). The court in In re Hawaii Federal Asbestos Cases (1986) said a "product's design is considered at the time of trial not the time of manufacture," in part because "Hawaii Rule of Evidence 407 allows the jury to consider subsequent remedial measures as proof of a defect."

It is apparent that the state-of-the-art concept is kaleidoscopic in meaning, and for that reason perhaps at least the position of the court in Karns v. Emerson Elec. Co. (1987), should be adopted: "While evidence bearing upon design alternatives and the 'state of the art' in the industry may be relevant to determining whether a product is unreasonably dangerous ... such evidence is not an essential element of the plaintiff's case." The court in Beshada v. Johns–Manville Prod. Corp. (1982) went even further in holding such evidence irrelevant in a strict tort case for failure to warn of the dangers of asbestos, because of the "vast confusion that is virtually certain to arise from any attempt to deal in a trial setting with the concept of scientific knowability." Accord, Carrecter v. Colson Equip. Co. (1985) ("no room" in strict liability case for negligence-based defense under the guise of state of the art).

## 5.   CODES, REPORTS, AND TECHNICAL LITERATURE

Safety codes drawn up by industry-sponsored associations are admissible on the issue of defectiveness, due care, and other disputed issues in a case. In Union Supply Co. v. Pust (1978), such standards were held admissible when "introduced through an expert witness" who was subject to cross-examination "on any inconsistencies, misrepresentations or other limitations of the standards." Such evidence can be considered without presenting the compilers of the codes as witnesses. Nordstrom v. White Metal Rolling & Stamping Corp. (1969). In Sterling v. Velsicol Chem. Corp. (1986), the expert witnesses relied on numerous manuals and guidelines published by both industry and the government regarding the proper methods of hazardous waste disposal. Industry safety codes are often treated as nonhearsay, since they represent "a consensus of opinion carrying the approval of a significant segment of an industry." McComish v. DeSoi (1964).

In Schmutz v. Bolles (1990) the court held that evidence of surgical drill malfunctions kept by the defendant manufacturer should have been admitted as business records to show causation and defectiveness. Although the evidence was derived from statements by outside parties, they had sufficient indicia of reliability because the defendant obtained the information from doctors and hospital representatives and relied on the reports to process repair and replacement requests. The ancient document rule (20 years) was held sufficient to authenticate the Summer–Simpson papers in Threadgill v. Armstrong World Industries (1991).

Government codes and regulations offered by expert witnesses are widely admitted to establish the elements of a products case. Pyatt v. Engel Equip., Inc. (1974). In Bunn v. Caterpillar Tractor Co. (1976), the court held that OSHA regulations were admissible against a product manufacturer on the issue of defectiveness, even though such regulations applied to employer conduct and not to product design. The jury was instructed that the evidence of these regulations "could be used to set up a standard if they so decided to use it," but that it was "not to be considered as binding" on the defendant.

The court in Ellsworth v. Sherne Lingerie, Inc. (1985) held that government investigative reports regarding the incidence of accidental fabric burn injuries were admissible not only as the basis for expert opinion but also as substantive evidence pursuant to the public records exception to the hearsay rule as embodied in Fed. R. Evid. 803(8).

The court noted that this exception is limited to "factual findings", but that the "line between 'fact' and 'opinion' is often difficult to draw.... Conclusions found in reports need not be judgmental.... Thus, attaching labels of 'fact' or 'opinion' or 'conclusion' will not necessarily resolve the issue, and careful attention must be given to the true nature of the statement and the totality of circumstances bearing on the ultimate issue of reliability." Similarly, in Kehm v. Proctor & Gamble Mfg. Co. (1983), the court admitted the results of an investigation by the Center of Disease Control to determine the relation between tampon use and toxic shock syndrome. Government reports, the court said, have often been admitted "setting forth agency opinions and conclusions on the ground that such reports, because they are public records based on investigations conducted pursuant to lawful authority, are presumptively reliable."

In Wells v. Ortho Pharmaceutical Corp. (1986), the plaintiffs' experts relied on numerous epidemiological studies to establish the causal relation between a spermicide and birth defects. The appellate court held this evidence was properly admitted, and the plaintiffs' verdict was supported by the evidence, even though the trial court found the conflicting studies "inconclusive" in this "battle of the experts" and was ultimately "forced to make credibility determinations to 'decide the victor'."

Learned treatises are admitted as an exception to the hearsay rule under Fed. R. Evid. 803(18):

To the extent called to the attention of an expert witness upon cross-examination or relied upon by him in direct examination, statements contained in published treatises, periodicals, or pamphlets on a subject of history, medicine, or other science or art, established as a reliable authority by the testimony or admission of the witness or by other expert testimony or by judicial notice. If admitted, the statements may be read into evidence but may not be received as exhibits.

The comment to this section recognizes that the "great weight of authority has been that learned treatises are not admissible as substantive evidence though usable in the cross-examination of experts" under varying rules of relevance. The federal rule adopts the "minority view", however, in recognition that such learned treatises are "written primarily and impartially for professionals, subject to scrutiny and exposure for inaccuracy, with the reputation of the writer at stake."

## 6.  DISCOVERY

The use and abuse of discovery have become controversial issues in civil litigation generally, including products liability. Some commentators believe discovery is used excessively, while others think that it is underutilized. Some courts may adopt rules restricting the use of discovery. A counterpart problem is that of stonewalling, where a litigant refuses to cooperate fairly in the discovery process. See Honda Motor Co. v. Salzman (1988) (liability imposed against defendant for wilful failure to comply with discovery orders).

A particularly sensitive area is where a blood recipient who has contracted AIDS from a blood transfusion seeks the names of blood donors, to determine the source of the AIDS virus, in a suit against a blood supplier for negligence in failing to detect the virus. Such discovery may be prohibited by statute, Irwin Memorial Blood Centers v. Superior Court (1991), or by court order, Belle Bonfils Mem. Blood Center v. Denver District Court (1988), in order to protect the privacy of the donor. Other courts allow such discovery. Most v. Tulane Medical Center (1991).

A court may issue a protective order, pursuant to Fed. R. Civ. Proc. 26(c) or its state counterpart, to protect a party from annoyance, embarrassment, oppression, or undue burden or expense. A protective order may also issue to protect a litigant's interest in confidentiality.

In Mampe v. Ayerst Laboratories (1988) the court held that a protective order could be issued on a showing of good cause after the granting of defendant's motion for summary judgment, to require the plaintiff to return to the defendant all confidential documents obtained through discovery and not made a part of the record. In Glasser v. A.H. Robins Co. (1991) (Dalkon Shield litigation) the court issued a protective order providing that persons authorized to examine closed files, in order to testify as plaintiffs' expert witness, could not disclose the contents of the files to persons outside the litigation without the court's permission.

# EPILOGUE

Products liability will undoubtedly continue to be a controversial field of law, because it cuts across so many fundamental issues in our society. It will also remain a simulating field of study and practice, since it combines a healthy mixture of the practical and the theoretical. The subject will certainly continue to change, both by statutory and by common law modification.

Products liability implicates many of the basic values of our society. It is a test of the ability of private industry to accommodate competitiveness and safety. It tests the fairness and the workability of the tort system of recovery, and of the jury system as a method of resolving disputes. It is perhaps not inappropriate to view the law of products liability as a microcosm and a distillation of the entire system of civil litigation in this country.

\*

# INDEX

**INCONSISTENT VERDICTS,** 167–168

**INDEMNITY**
Active-passive, 118
Attorney fees, 118
Economic loss, 119–120
Implied warranty, 117
Partial liability, 118–119
Settlements, 122
Statute of limitations, 184
Vicarious liability, 117

**JOINT AND SEVERAL LIABILITY**
Comparative fault, 274–276
Policy for, 80–81
Statutory changes, 81–82
Unif. Compar. Fault Act, 82

**JURISDICTION**
Class actions, 163–166
Minimum contacts, 159–163
Statutory causes of action, 157–159

**LESSOR**
See Defendants

**LICENSOR**
See Defendants, subheading Lessor, bailor, or licensor

**MERCHANT**
Express warranty, not required, 64
Fitness, not required, 55
Rest. 2d of Torts § 402A, p. 56–57
Rest. 2d of Torts § 402B, p. 66–69
UCC § 2–314, pp. 51–52

**MIDDLEMAN**
Auctioneer, 93–94
Broker, 91–93
Pharmacist, 91
Retailer, 89–90
Sealed container doctrine, 90
Wholesaler, 91

**MILITARY CONTRACTOR DEFENSE**
See Contract Specifications Defense

†